Neuro-Discipline:
Everyday Neuroscience for Self-Discipline, Focus, and Defeating Your Brain's Impulsive and Distracted Nature

By Peter Hollins,
Author and Researcher at
petehollins.com

Table of Contents

Chapter 1. The Neuroscience of Self-Discipline 7
A Tale of Two Brains 10
Give Me What I Want 19
The Speed of Self-Discipline 29
The Essence of Sacrifice 38

Chapter 2. Trick the Brain 51
Me, Myself, and I 53
Behavior Chains 63
Pleasure Now, Pleasure Later 70
Smaller, Faster, Closer 75

Chapter 3. Trick the Brain Pt. 2 97
Deconstruct Pleasure 98
Environmental Assistance 106
Shift Your Focus 123

Chapter 4. Mind Shift 139
What Did You Say to Me? 142
Know Your Style 152
Excuses, Excuses 159

Chapter 5. Creating Space and Calm 177
Delay, Delay, Delay 178
Keep Your Mind 188
The Master of Discomfort 196

Summary Guide 215

Chapter 1. The Neuroscience of Self-Discipline

Kate had always wanted to learn French, but she was having some problems. It wasn't just the pronunciation or reading comprehension; she wasn't even at that point yet. She was unable to carve out time in her schedule to even learn how to order a croissant and coffee.

Her daily schedule looked something like the following:

8:30 a.m. to 5:00 p.m.: Work

5:30 p.m. to 7:00 p.m.: Exercise or meet a friend for coffee

7:30 to 9: 30 p.m.: Eat dinner and watch television or meet a friend for dinner

9:30 to 11:00 p.m.: Unwind from the day, update social media, and catch up on gossip from friends

11:30 p.m.: Time for sleep

One day over lunch, she put this schedule into writing and showed it to a friend she was complaining to about not being able to achieve her goals with French. *How could she ever make time to learn French? She was so busy!* Her friend took a moment to consider how he wanted to spend the next 30 minutes of his life and then simply agreed with Kate that it was too difficult, and they had a pleasant and nondescript lunch together.

In reality, all of us are Kate at some point or another. We have goals, whether lofty or low, that we can't seem to reach. It feels like it's out of our power, and it might even feel like a fantasy. Is it actually true that Kate is destined to be monolingual and have her dreams of retiring in rural France dashed to the ground? No, but it's not her fault if that's her starting point.

We're not excusing laziness or letting our goals fall by the wayside, but we do need to acknowledge that our brains are simply programmed to do as little work as possible, seek maximum pleasure, and generally bask in the sun like a house cat. Kate is just an illustration of how our brains are the opposite of goal-oriented, except when it comes to instant gratification and the fulfillment of only short-term pleasures—for her, these are exercising, eating, and socializing with friends. She is unwilling to delay or sacrifice what she wants (these daily pleasures), so she remains stuck in place, though very comfortable.

Much of what we will discuss in this book is either directly or indirectly designed to battle our own brains and rise above our natural instincts. This is the actual neuroscience of self-discipline, motivation, and getting things done. The same instincts that make us human are the ones that make us binge eat, act against our own best interests, and keep us firmly rooted in a place that we don't want.

A Tale of Two Brains

These struggles all start from the way that our brains have developed over time, and understanding our brain's basic structure will provide mental orientation. We have to pay attention to two components in particular.

The *cerebral cortex* is probably the most recognizable part of the brain, as we've seen the brain depicted in biology textbooks—the gray matter that physically resembles a thick sponge. The cerebral cortex is the processor of thought, reason, language, and general consciousness. It may help to assign a so-called avatar to each portion of the brain, and since this portion is focused on analytical thought, this is the *Albert Einstein* portion. The cerebral cortex is further divided into four subcomponents called *lobes*, but we are only concerned with the frontal lobe. Thus, we typically refer to the prefrontal cortex.

The prefrontal cortex is probably where most of us "exist" in our minds: the conscious and analytical part of us that makes choices based on the information we've obtained. It's basically the hub of "free will" and our personality development, including decision-making, planning, and thought and analysis. It's like the conference room of the mind.

The prefrontal cortex is where we try to organize our behavior and thoughts with the goals we've set up. It's typically associated with "executive function"—where we make judgments and decisions and formulate strategies to align our actions with our "beliefs," like moral or value judgments (good vs. bad, better vs. best), qualitative assessments (similarities and differences), consequential thinking (what will happen if certain actions are taken, what's the predicted outcome), and social behavior. Specifically, the ventral medial and dorsolateral prefrontal cortex show increased activity when engaging in tasks that require self-discipline and thinking about long-term consequences.

We use the prefrontal cortex to predict stock market rises, strategize marriage proposals, figure out if we're going to dress up as a goth, and decide where to get lunch. As you might suspect, this is the part of the brain where self-discipline lives. But just like Albert Einstein, it is frail and not very strong. The component responsible for holding poor Albert Einstein in a figurative chokehold is the *limbic system*.

The limbic system is an umbrella term for all the structures that govern our emotions, stress responses, and instinctual drives for sex and hunger, for instance. As you again may have suspected, it's often the part of our brain that we want to shut off because it is behind our lack of self-discipline. Simply put, if we are unable to regulate our drives or impulses, or are ruled by our emotions, then thinking critically and analytically becomes nearly impossible. The limbic system thinks it is still the year 10,000 BC and hasn't updated itself despite the world around it changing dramatically.

A useful avatar for the limbic system is a skittish cat that runs and hides first and foremost. There's no thinking, only a reaction based on a desire to fulfill some unconscious instinct. And just like the cat, the limbic system becomes fierce and dangerous if it feels caged. Sometimes it will do nearly anything to run and hide.

The limbic system is always watching out for us, which is great in theory, but it can also be unnecessarily restrictive. Imagine how phobias and anxiety can derail you despite your best intentions—those are both the result of the limbic system not being adequately balanced by the prefrontal cortex. Both the prefrontal cortex and the limbic system very badly want to make our decisions for us, and as such, they're frequently battling each other for that responsibility. It's your good old-fashioned conflict between logic and emotion.

This struggle is what makes self-discipline so difficult. As your prefrontal cortex is making evidence- and logic-based decisions, your limbic system hijacks that process with its emotional response. Kate sought out the emotional responses of comfort and pleasure, and those were drives that were ultimately too strong for her to overcome. The limbic system's pursuit of pleasure and/or relief can be so powerful that it will overwhelm the supreme reason of the prefrontal cortex, driving one to make unfortunate choices.

For instance, you are probably already familiar with one facet of the limbic system that makes us completely incapable of reasoned thought: the *fight-or-flight* response. This occurs whenever the brain encounters a frightening situation and is forced to decide whether to stay and confront the problem or get the heck out of Dodge and seek safety. The fight-or-flight response emerges from several different kinds of threats: an oncoming car (flight), a stovetop kitchen fire (fight, hopefully), a snarling attack dog (could go either way), or a vindictive father-in-law knocking at your door with a shotgun (you're on your own). It even emerges from things like becoming irrationally angry when someone is late or if someone calls you by a nickname that you dislike.

In a suddenly stressful situation, the body releases hormones that signal the body's sympathetic nervous system, which alerts the adrenal system to release hormones that spur the chemical production of adrenaline or noradrenaline. This causes the body to feel certain physical symptoms (high blood pressure, increased heart and breathing rates). The body doesn't return to "normal" until between 20 and 60 minutes after the threat goes away.

The fight-or-flight response is another way that the limbic system ultimately helps us, but it also presents certain drawbacks. It doesn't differentiate between *actual* threats and just *perceived* ones. It also reacts to the fear of completely unrealistic events: the recurrence of diseases that have been cured, a swarm of killer bees, a zombie apocalypse, or a piano falling from a tall building. These just don't happen, not even the zombie apocalypse. And the limbic system's inaccuracy about such potential events is what leads to the development of phobias, which have an oversized influence on the super-reasonable prefrontal cortex.

A helpful representation of the brain comes in the form of the triune brain theory, developed by neuroscientist Paul MacLean in the 1960s. It's not what most modern neuroscientists would use, but it can clearly illustrate what self-discipline is battling.

Roughly put, the triune brain theory assigns every human three brains (congratulations). Two of them are the brain regions we've already discussed: the prefrontal cortex (Albert Einstein) and the limbic system (skittish cat).

The first "brain" was described by MacLean as the *neomammalian complex*—what we've described as the prefrontal cortex ("neo" means new). In his view, this structure is exclusive only to so-called "higher" mammals, like human beings and other very closely related primates. It gives us our capacity for thought and consciousness, language, planning, and so forth. Unfortunately, this is not where our priorities lie.

The second "brain" is the *paleomammalian complex*, or what we've discussed as the overall limbic system ("paleo" means older). As the name implies, MacLean likened this part of the brain to prehistoric mammals that didn't have much immediate need for reflection or deep understanding—they just needed to feed themselves, procreate, and watch after the children. But they needed to have a sensation that spurred these activities on: to eat, they needed to feel hungry. So the paleomammalian complex reflects those primal urges: hunger, sexual arousal, parental drive, and the emotions they call up. This is where our priorities lie, much of the time outside of our conscious awareness.

The third "brain" is the *reptilian complex*. It's so named because scientists used to believe that reptiles were driven by raw instinct more than carefully considered need and biological imperative. We're talking domination and aggressive attacks on other species, territorial marking, and ceremonial acts (like a peacock showing its plumage).

The triune brain theory states that these three "brains" are always at each other's, well, throats. Your rational, advanced human brain knows full well that it needs to do certain very practical things and that if you do them fully, you'll more likely get positive results. But the caveman-like paleomammalian brain is always interrupting the prefrontal cortex with its primitive urges and emotions. And when you throw the reptile brain on top, with its raw hunger and savagery, forget it—all your best-laid plans are now in utter chaos. The self-discipline you want requires your neomammalian brain to constantly win, but that's tough to accomplish.

Another way to think about the arrangement of the brains is in terms of energy expenditure. The prefrontal cortex needs a lot of gas to do its work. You have to constantly call up the reserves to think thoroughly about a situation, ponder the pros and cons, create something, predict an outcome—it's literally brainpower, and you need it to think things through. No one wants to do this for every decision, especially ones that appear to require speed. The limbic system, on the other hand, is almost automatic. It takes nothing to process emotions or instantaneously react out of mere instinct. The limbic system loves the path of least resistance because it's easier and takes less energy to maintain. The reptilian complex falls somewhere in between.

Once again, the introduction of the triune brain is for illustrative purposes only. It's meant to show why our actions don't match our intentions and how our brains work against us in many cases. Just as it's in us to remain at home and only indulge in our primal drives, it is also in us to do what we need to achieve our goals.

Give Me What I Want

When we think about Kate now, can we draw a slightly different conclusion about her decidedly un-busy schedule and subsequent inability to learn French? We might say that her limbic system's drives were simply too powerful for her prefrontal cortex to overcome. She was a victim of her emotional drives or comfort, security, and a lack of challenge or stress. In the battle for her behaviors, the skittish cat won out far more often than Mr. Einstein.

But beyond the two battling structures, we also come to the neurotransmitter *dopamine* and how that also helps determine our self-disciplined (or not) behaviors. The brain is a network. It's fundamentally composed of nerve cells, or neurons. These neurons communicate to each other through chemical reactions—an impulse in one nerve fiber gets activated, then is converted into a chemical that flies across the gap and is received by another nerve fiber. This act, multiplied by about a trillion times a day, basically controls everything we do, say, or think, one way or another.

That chemical that's flying across the gap is called a neurotransmitter, and different neurotransmitters are responsible for different communications to the brain. Self-discipline is especially tied to a specific neurotransmitter: dopamine.

That's because dopamine is one of the agents that work on the brain's pleasure and reward centers. It's especially tied to the mesolimbic pathway, the most vital reward pathway in the human brain, located near its center.

In other words, when we experience pleasure or a reward of some type, dopamine is usually at the root of it—the greater the amount of dopamine released, the greater the pleasure we feel. It happens during and after a pleasurable event—you feel it *while* you are eating a dozen donuts and also *after* you finish a great workout at the gym. However, dopamine is also released in *anticipation* of pleasure or reward, which ties it directly to motivation. Kate feels dopamine while exercising, anticipating her social media binge, and after meeting with a friend. She's trapped—and why wouldn't she seek to imbue her day with as much pleasure as possible?

If you start feeling good in anticipation of something, chances are you will be motivated into action to seek more of it. However, we unconsciously seek dopamine in our daily lives, and sometimes this pursuit creates self-sabotage in the form of laziness, sloth, distraction, and lack of focus. Discipline, of course, is more or less the definition of a *lack* of dopamine.

Dopamine's role in reinforcing pleasure correlates to one of the most well-known theories concerning human behavior. Rather, perhaps it's more accurate to say that the studies on dopamine align with this more foundational theory. This is the pleasure principle, and it simply states that the human mind does everything it can to seek out pleasure and avoid pain. It doesn't get simpler than that. In that simplicity, we find some of life's most universal and predictable motivators.

Every decision we make is based on gaining pleasure or avoiding pain. This is the common motivation for every person on earth. No matter what we do in the course of our day, it all gets down to the pleasure principle. You raid the refrigerator for snacks because you crave the taste and feel of certain food. You get a haircut because you think it will make you more attractive to someone else, which will make you happy, which is pleasure.

Conversely, you wear a protective mask while you're using a blowtorch because you want to avoid sparks flying into your face and eyes, because that would be painful. If you trace all of our decisions back, whether short term or long term, you'll find that they all stem from a small set of pleasures or pains.

People work harder to avoid pain than to get pleasure. While everyone wants pleasure as much as they can get it, their motivation to avoid pain is actually far stronger. The instinct to survive a threatening situation is more immediate than eating your favorite candy bar, for instance. So when faced with the prospect of pain, the brain will work harder than it would to gain access to pleasure.

For example, imagine you're standing in the middle of a desert road. In front of you is a treasure chest filled with money and outlandishly expensive jewelry that could set you up financially for the rest of your life. But there's also an out-of-control semi careening toward it. You're probably going to make the decision to jump away from the truck rather than grab the treasure chest, because your instinct to avoid pain—in this case, certain death—outweighed your desire to gain pleasure.

Our perceptions of pleasure and pain are more powerful drivers than the actual things. When our brain is judging between what will be a pleasant or painful experience, it's working from scenarios that we *think* could result if we took a course of action. In other words, our *perceptions* of pleasure and pain are really what's driving the cart. And sometimes those perceptions can be flawed. In fact, they are mostly flawed, which explains our tendency to work against our own best interests.

For Kate, the thought of retiring in rural France is attractive, but the perception of how difficult and time-consuming learning French will be is quite a scary thought for her. How difficult is learning a new language? Well, it's not easy. But she doesn't have firsthand knowledge of it, and she just imagines that she will be terrible at it.

Pleasure and pain are changed by time. In general, we focus on the here and now: what can I get very soon that will bring me happiness? Also, what is coming up very soon that could be intensely painful and I'll have to avoid? When considering the attainment of comfort, we're more tuned into what might happen immediately. The pleasure and pain that might happen months or years from now doesn't really register with us—what's most important is whatever's right at our doorstep. Of course, this is another reason that our self-discipline suffers. We can't keep the future in mind when the present is so distracting.

For example, a smoker needs a cigarette. It's the main focus of their current situation. It brings them a certain relief or pleasure. And in about fifteen minutes, they'll be on break so they can enjoy that cigarette. It's the focus of their daily ritual. They're *not* thinking about how smoking a cigarette every time they "need" one could cause painful health problems down the road.

That's a distant reality that's not driving them at all. Right now, they need a smoke because they crave one, and they might get a headache immediately if they don't get one.

Emotion beats logic. When it comes to the pleasure principle, your feelings tend to overshadow rational thought. You might know that doing something will be good or bad for you. You'll understand all the reasons why it will be good or bad. You'll get all that. But if you are so intent on satisfying a certain craving, then it's probably going to win out.

Going back to our smoker, without a doubt they know why cigarettes are bad for one's health. They've read those warnings on the packages. Maybe in school they saw a picture of a corroded lung that resulted from years of smoking. They *know* all the risks they're about to court. But there's that pack right in front of them. And all reason be damned, they're going to have that cigarette. Their emotions oriented toward pleasure win out.

The pleasure principle is related to an idea that comes from economics and the attempt to predict markets and human buying behavior: the *rational choice theory*, embodied by the jokingly named *Homo economicus*. This states that all of our choices and decisions spring entirely from self-interest and the desire to bring as much pleasure to our lives as possible. It may not always hold up (otherwise, market and stock prices would be 100% predictable), but it provides more support for the simple nature of many of our motivations.

With all this in mind, it stands to reason that if we can cleverly manipulate the amount of dopamine we create in our brains, we can be more self-disciplined. Since things as small as scrolling through social media can generate dopamine, this is easier than we think. We'll discuss specific tactics and strategies later on. For now, the absence of dopamine from the actions that underlie our goals is a piece of the puzzle of inaction.

But there's even more to setting yourself up for self-disciplined success, and this time it's about making sure that our emotional state will allow for it. Only then can we truly utilize our rational brains.

Plainly put, if you are in any state of stress, anxiety, or overwhelm, then you are pretty much primed for self-disciplined failure. We can illustrate this with one simple question: if you've just worked 12 hours in a row, are you going to make the choice to cook a healthy meal, or will you be slightly more susceptible to eating fast food? If we're stressed, we cease to think clearly and are back to our primal states of satisfying urges and drives. We can't regulate ourselves. A brain on excessive stress is a brain in crisis mode.

Control quite literally shifts from the prefrontal cortex to the limbic system and engages the fight-or-flight instinct. Cortisol, the stress hormone, is released, as well as constant amounts of adrenaline. Both of those hormones prevent you from quick thinking and keep you in a state of high alertness and reactivity. Prolonged and frequent stress also affects our memory retention, makes it more difficult to sleep, and has actually been shown to shrink the size of our brains. At this point, an unfortunate cycle begins, and the stress grows and grows.

Our bodies don't know what stresses we are facing, but it just knows that we are distressed, and it wants to help. Self-preservation is its only function, and it does whatever it needs to do to make that transpire.

The Speed of Self-Discipline

So, given all this, it should start to seem clear that the brain is simply not wired for discipline. Because of the way our neurotransmitters and brain structures have evolved over time, human beings are primed to take the path of least resistance almost all the time. Our emotions are "faster" than our more logical, rational thought and will always jump ahead and influence us if we don't take specific action to respect our slower, more reasonable responses.

What do we do with this knowledge of how our brains function? The point is not to see any aspect of the mind as "wrong", but rather to be aware of its limitations and act to moderate them, refusing to prioritize knee-jerk emotional responses that only serve to keep us in a reactive, unconscious state.

Thus we come to our general principle in living a more self-disciplined life and battling our limbic brain and absence of dopamine: act *before* your emotional monkey mind can jump in and try to stop you with complaints, fears, or laziness. Given enough time, your monkey mind can convince you of nearly anything. A great way to think about this inner conflict in the mind is to use Mel Robbins' now-famous Five Second Rule.

The rule is pretty straightforward: the moment you feel an impulse to act toward achieving a goal, have the discipline to act *within the next five seconds*. Simply stop, acknowledge that you're about to make a decision, then count down silently in your head: "five, four, three…" When you hit zero (or before), act.

What's the rush? Well, Robbins understands that this five-second window period is crucial. It's the tiny gap you get before your mind steps in and finds excuses for you or jeopardizes you with indecision or fear. The simple act of counting alone also focuses the mind and pushes out all that mental traffic that typically hurries in to paralyze us, undermining the original impulse to act.

You don't give yourself time to dwell on your excuses, your avoidance, your doubts—you just act. Though this might seem like a rash approach to many, the Five Second Rule is about striking while the iron is hot. If you wait longer than five seconds? Your mind has the chance to jump in with all your same old excuses and worries. And then you never act. But act swiftly and you give your prefrontal human brain priority, well before the emotional limbic brain can barge in and help you procrastinate, dawdle, or self-sabotage.

Let's take a closer look at each element of this rule. First, your instinct or impulse here is not a rash choice that could harm yourself or others, and it's not anything that's illegal or irresponsible. We're not talking about the decision to jump off a bridge or suddenly quit your job during a heated argument with your boss.

Rather, "instinct" here is all about what you know to be the correct or best action. Your gut feeling tells you that something is right, and the pull of that can be incredibly strong and clear. These moments of wisdom and clarity, however, can be fleeting. They speak louder than the compulsion to procrastinate or avoid, but once the machinery for fear and denial kicks in, that voice can be squashed.

Secondly, in this model, instincts are those to *act toward a specific goal*. Instincts are not vague and pointless—they emerge in us as a response to deeply held desires and goals we want to achieve. You might not be consciously aware yet of the action you need to take, but your unconscious mind may well synthesize everything for you and present you with an irresistible impulse in the moment.

Thirdly, even though the action is toward a self-identified goal and even though your intuition is strongly nudging you toward it, you must still push yourself to act. You might not "want to," but the fact is, nothing will happen if you wait until you feel like acting. Accept the fact that being out of your comfort zone and doing something scary or difficult is the cost of growth. Luckily, with this rule, you don't have to argue or convince yourself or weigh up pros and cons. You just act. Now.

Fourth, your action needs to be physical. Move in the direction your intuition is urging you to. Send an email, speak up, call a friend, get up off the sofa to go to the gym, or put down your unhealthy snack. Whatever it is, act and make a difference in your world before the critical window closes and your brain stops you.

Finally, act knowing that if you let the window close, your mind will rush in and destroy your dreams. All your irrational, overly fearful, and lazy mental programs will start again on autopilot. Your fears and doubts will prevent you from growing as a person and taking risks, and once they've set in properly, they simply convince you they're protecting you, and change will never happen.

Step in before your mind convinces you that growth is dangerous. Outsmart your brain by acting before it can react this way. As an example, consider a woman with a goal to be more assertive. She hears someone talking in a meeting about a topic she's an expert in, and she feels an impulse to speak up and share her opinion. Before her monkey mind can convince her that this is a bad idea, she counts down to five and opens her mouth.

This method rests on the idea that you already know what's right—you're just getting out of your own way in order to act according to what you know. It's about not giving your primitive, fearful mind the chance to undermine your more conscious, rational goals.

There's plenty of research to support the idea that the older, more primitive, and emotional parts of our brains work quicker than our more recently evolved prefrontal cortices, or logical brains. A Canadian study has shown that it takes mere fractions of a second for our brains to process emotional information compared to much slower times to process abstract verbal information.

Simply put, we pay more attention to material that is purely emotional, especially if it's based on fear or anger. Because it was evolutionarily advantageous to do so throughout our history as a species, the brain puts this kind of content at the front of the processing queue, prioritizing survival above all else. But this also means that fears and phobias, even when they aren't relevant, will be at the front of the mind. If we want to push ourselves past our evolutionary limits, we need to get into the habit of recognizing when these ancient fears crop up and acting quickly before they have a chance to derail us.

Mel Robbins isn't the only one to recognize the power of letting your gut intuitions act quickly before your fear can stop you. A related technique is called the "Samurai seven breaths." Essentially, one should strive to make decisions within the span of seven breaths, no longer.

It originated from feudal Japan, where Lord Takandobu says of making decisions, "If discrimination is long, it will spoil." Lord Naoshige went on to say in the *Hagakure*, "When matters are done leisurely, seven out of ten will turn out badly. A warrior is a person who does things quickly. When your mind is going hither and thither, discrimination will never be brought to a conclusion. With an intense, fresh and undelaying spirit, one will make his judgments within the space of seven breaths. It is a matter of being determined and having the spirit to break right through to the other side."

We see the same recommendation here: act quickly and in line with your deeply felt goals and intuitions, well before doubt, fear, and laziness can crop up and hold you back. The truth is that when it comes to a goal that is truly important to you, you already know what the correct course of action is. It doesn't take hours to deliberate on it—you feel it instantly. However, negative self-talk, procrastination, and excuses can all take their time and fill any moments of deliberation with more and more reasons not to act. Using either the Five Second Rule or the seven breaths rule is an elegant way to side-step all of that and give your rational mind a chance to work toward making your dreams a reality.

So, now that you understand the biology and the evolutionary history of the amazing and yet flawed thing called your brain, what next? What does this imply for self-discipline? Where does this leave us in practical terms and how we can approach it?

The Essence of Sacrifice

The concept of sacrifice is not something that most people want to delve into, let alone become good at. Yet sacrifice is at the core of self-discipline. There are many, many things (conscious and unconscious) that we must choose to let go of if we are to achieve our goals with discipline. Staying exactly where you are takes no effort. But to achieve a goal, you need to realistically accept the fact that the way out of your current state is through a degree of discomfort. In other words, you must give up what you want *now* for what you want *most*. We revisit Kate one last time as the prime example of someone who didn't want to sacrifice anything in her current lifestyle. Without sacrifice she remained motionless and far away from her goals.

It may seem strange to look at all the things you can't have in order to achieve what you want, but this focus and hard work is an unavoidable part of practicing self-discipline. Just don't be surprised and let it throw you off track. A feeling of deprivation is bound to be everywhere when you start, and it's often the sign that things are going correctly.

Let go of perfectionism. Lofty goals in the future can immobilize you. Instead, think of small, incremental ways to improve bit by bit, day by day. There's no such thing as perfect, and striving for it is pointless. However, you *can* always improve on yesterday. In each passing moment, resist the urge to compare yourself to a perfect, complete end goal. Instead, ask, "Am I going in the right direction here? Am I growing now or am I stalling?" Getting started is better than being perfect. Start, even though you can't be guaranteed of success.

Let go of wanting silver bullets. We've all bought into the idea that there's one quick fix, one magic pill, or one bright moment that carries us over into the realm of success. But success takes time. It takes consistent effort; it's more like an endless string of steady gains than one big leap into achievement. Wanting a quick-fix is a sign of fear and laziness. There is no such thing as overnight success: we only see the impressive end product of a successful person's entire lifetime of effort. You'll have to do the same.

Let go of FOMO—fear of missing out. There's no nice way to say it: you can't "have it all." Achieving a goal means focus, and when you are focused on something, you necessarily turn attention away from everything else. Choose wisely. Commitment means the inner dedication to taking that *one* path that you know and trust to be the most worthwhile and meaningful for you. It comes back to sacrifice. Are you willing to sacrifice a handful of mediocre moments for one glorious one? A lifetime of less important things for the few things that truly matter to you?

Let go of people-pleasing. Life goals, especially those big, serious ones that speak right to our soul, have nothing to do with anyone else. It's impossible to please anyone, and it's never your job in any case. Trust that others are on their own mission and that you're on yours. Realize that this means that on occasion, people will be unhappy with you or make you a villain in their own story. When you have a goal that truly matters, you can easily be authentic and do what *you* believe is right.

Let go of people who don't encourage your growth. We're all on different paths in life. Are the people you have in your life helping your growth and development, or are they actively working against it? Ask yourself whether your friends and family inspire you to be better or teach you or support you. Invest your time in people that are in line with your future self.

Let go of multitasking. This comes back to focus. Your brain can only process one task at a time anyway, so choose that task, commit to it, and focus on getting it done. Distraction, task-flipping, and juggling only make you more inefficient—and more stressed. Every day, tiny distractions will creep into your every passing moment. Discipline means sacrificing the urge to constantly check your phone, lose your train of thought, or ditch a task before it's finished.

Let go of "I'll do it later." Procrastination will kill your dreams like nothing else. This is our monkey mind again, spinning tales of fear that prevent us from taking action. If you are disorganized, commit, right now, to organizing yourself. If fear is holding you back (fear of failure or of success!), act quickly, before you talk yourself out of it. If you "don't feel like it," well, so what? The big sacrifice here is not really a sacrifice at all: wouldn't you rather have your goal than another pointless afternoon spent wasting time online?

Let go of old excuses. The best way to know your emotional monkey mind is steering the ship is to notice the lengths you go to explain to yourself why you can't grow or take action. An excuse is a nonsense "reason" your fear makes up to defend inaction and avoid responsibility. It feels comfortable but ultimately is self-defeating. At the bottom of every excuse is "I'm afraid." But you can consciously decide that fear is not a reason to give up on your goals.

Let go of control. This may seem counterintuitive. Isn't goal-setting all about control? Yes and no. When you focus and commit to a goal, you are naturally more enthusiastic and positive. You don't need to control others around you when you can control yourself, your actions, and your attitude. Refuse to waste energy on things that are not in your zone of control. Pour it instead into the places you truly can make a difference—your attitude, right now.

Let go of preconceptions. You're the one telling the story. Your mind tells you what is possible and what isn't. That's why it's so important to challenge yourself if you're deliberately closing yourself into a narrow worldview and being closed-minded. Adopt an attitude of curiosity and always be willing to learn—i.e., to prove yourself wrong! Don't hold onto pet notions and beliefs too tightly. After all, your beliefs may be the very thing keeping you where you don't want to be. Get into the habit of questioning everything, including your own biases. Don't be afraid, above all, to *change your mind*.

Let go of instant gratification. When you focus solely on short-term goals, you may sabotage those longer-term ones. Guilty pleasures in the moment may "solve" immediate needs but do nothing for tomorrow. Ask whether your actions now are working for your future self. You might have a desire right in front of you and a desire that only kicks in when you're 70 years old. Keep both in mind when you act. Remind yourself that what you do today is setting the conditions for tomorrow. Do you want to help your future self or undermine them?

Let go of being unhealthy. All this talk of the mind makes goal-setting seem abstract. However, your brain is a part of your body, just like your heart and stomach. When you are in poor health, it doesn't matter how lofty your goals are or how much self-discipline you can muster. Have respect for your physical body and never sacrifice your well-being for a goal—instead, think of nurturing your health as an investment in any goal you have. Eat well, exercise, and sleep properly, and you are in the best possible position to achieve the goals you want to.

Let go of the need for security. Our primitive minds evolved over the years to avoid risk and danger and move toward safety (i.e., what's already known). Unfortunately, this "comfort zone" is also a space where no growth or exploration can take place. Evolution takes risk and discomfort. What you gain in stability you lose in potential growth—you stagnate, letting opportunity fly by. No one is in charge of your life but you; if you want something wonderful for yourself, you have to sacrifice the (illusion of) safety and do something new and different. Afraid of failing? What's so bad about failing, anyway?

Let go of pushing yourself too hard. "No pain no gain" only applies up to a point. It's smart to rest often, giving yourself time to regenerate and also to passively, unconsciously process what you've learned. Frequent breaks can help you solve problems far quicker than hammering away at a task until you're exhausted. Give tricky problems over to your unconscious mind once in a while. Remember to enjoy life, to relax, and trust the process without beating yourself up.

Let go of… giving up. If you're working on a goal that's truly important to you, and you're putting in the time and effort every day, sooner or later you're going to reach a crisis point. You may want to give up when challenges seem too overwhelming or when you can't muster the energy anymore. Giving up on a goal that no longer serves you is one thing, but often the impulse to throw in the towel comes from fear and laziness.

Instead, pause and remind yourself of why you're pursuing your goal. What will the next five years look like if you give up now? And what about if you decide to push through your resistance and keep going? Be honest and ask whether you're wanting to quit because you're lazy and fearful or wanting to take the easy way out. You can always quit tomorrow, if you really want to. But quitting when you really should have carried on is harder to come back from.

Moments like these are gold: they invite us to dig deep and get really familiar with not just our fears and personal demons, but also the heart of what we're trying to build or create for ourselves. This is the zone where character is made and dreams are forged. These struggles are what will make you look back with pride. These difficult periods are the very thing that your growth and development are made of. Can you get excited about the person you'll be if you can push through this?

Takeaways:

- The neuroscience of self-discipline is really a tale of two brains. We have one brain, our more primitive and survival-focused brain, which simply makes us react for speed. It is fearful, high-strung, and not ultimately that smart. It's the limbic system, which we can also see as a skittish cat. Then we have our rational and thinking brain, the one which is capable of analyzing information and responding for accuracy rather than speed. This brain, while not always smart, is what allows self-discipline to occur. It is the prefrontal cortex, which we can see as Mr. Albert Einstein. Einstein and the skittish cat are constantly battling each other for supremacy, and it's up to us to make sure that the cat loses more often than not.

- Another large aspect of being biologically wired against self-discipline comes in the form of the pleasure principle. This principle simply states that humans are predisposed to seeking pleasure and avoiding pain, heavily reinforced by the neurotransmitter dopamine. This process hijacks our brain and makes discipline difficult, as it is the polar opposite of the pleasure principle; it is immediate discomfort and only long-term pleasure.

- We thus come to the realization that our brains are scared and lazy. Meanwhile, self-discipline is a process that requires an amount of awareness and rational thought. One way to think about this is through the Five Second Rule, in which self-disciplined action is best done within five seconds, or else primitive emotions are able to take us off course. It kicks us into motion before our brains, which are wired for fear and laziness, hold us back.
- Finally, a note on the mindset of self-discipline. We've been through the neuroscience, but we must touch on the concept of sacrifice. At its core, self-discipline is sacrifice and letting go. It is feeling discomfort, pushing past boundaries, and doing more than you ever did before. Those feelings, combined with deprivation, are the signs that you are on the right path.

Chapter 2. Trick the Brain

Now that we've got the pesky neuroscience out of the way, we can begin to discuss exactly what we can do to combat our lazy habits and dispositions. The first chapter was entirely necessary because if we know the true causes of our lack of self-discipline and not the simple symptoms, we can be far more effective. In truth, all of the tactics take these true causes into mind.

This chapter focuses specifically on ways to trick the brain into action. Recall that the brain has a few particular tendencies that we uncovered in the first chapter. It would be prudent to keep these in mind, because in one way or another, each of the subsequent tactics in this book will be battling one or more of them.

Let's call them *the imperatives of the brain (that we must defeat)*:

- The brain is locked in an epic battle with itself, between the instinct for the quickest reaction (emotion) and the most optimal reaction (logic).
- The brain wants as much pleasure as possible, as fast as possible; an absence of pain and discomfort will also do in most cases.
- Speed is of the essence for the brain.
- The brain never wants to sacrifice anything pleasurable.

The brain really sounds like a grumpy infant, if not a skittish cat. Indeed, every approach ultimately tries to slow the brain down, insert logic and reason, satisfy the pleasure principle in alternate ways, and put sacrifice in the context of greater life goals.

When we are tricking the brain, we aren't necessarily seeking to change the brain's tendencies (good luck with that) but instead are going around them.

Me, Myself, and I

We've talked about two brains, and now we talk about two *selves*. We start with the person that we fixate our thoughts on. Of course, we are naturally self-centered and fixate our thoughts on ourselves: what we will get out of something, how we will benefit, and how happy we will be.

But our natural instinct is to only fixate on ourselves in the present sense instead of how the *you of tomorrow* will feel. This is all too easy to see in many, many contexts. If we are in a poor mood, our wallets are instantly at high risk for overspending. If we are at an all-you-can-eat buffet, you better believe that you are going to get your money's worth. If a salesperson flatters your curves, then you are going to indulge yourself in something that is probably out of your budget. It happens whenever we are making a decision without thinking about what happens after, which is really our natural habit.

When we are exposed to instances where we can exercise self-discipline, we falter because we are stuck in the present moment with our present self. We are seduced by the pleasure principle, but in one specific way: we are focused only on our short-term pleasure, not long-term. This is what makes us unable to get off the couch, stop eating, or finish an extra batch of emails.

One solution for this is to "time travel," as Dr. Timothy Pychyl phrases it.

Don't worry: this book hasn't taken a turn to sci-fi-ville. Time travel here pertains to the practice of projecting yourself into the future. This should be motivating because it will become clear that certain actions will make you feel wonderful and others only full of regret. Vividly think about your future self and how they will feel. Think about how you want to help them be happier and work less. We might think about future consequences from time to time, but giving life to your future self is not something that is natural.

They are you, so don't you want to set themselves up to succeed in the present moment? Of course you do. When you can associate your present and impulsive actions with longer-term consequences, suddenly you gain perspective on what you should or shouldn't be doing. Visualize your future and all the positive and negative consequences that arise from a small, immediate action. Use your imagination.

For example, if you're not feeling motivated to work on a speech you've been asked to do, picture yourself already up on that podium in the heat of the moment. How would it go if you went into it well-prepared? What kind of applause would you receive, and how many accolades might you garner afterward? How satisfying is the feeling of a job well done, especially if it was a challenge?

On the other hand, how might you sound if you failed to prepare for it well enough? How red would your face be if you were stumbling for words, and how much brow sweat would accumulate? How might a poor performance change people's perceptions of you? Soak in that feeling of anxiety and panic.

Boy, there's a lot of pain or pleasure at stake from this one small action, isn't there? Picture the pains and the triumphs and use them as a mental boost. Admittedly, the pains will probably be more motivating, but that's okay. In small doses, pushing yourself using fear is a necessary evil.

The ultimate question in the end becomes, *if you wanted to treat your future self the best, how would you change your behavior in the present*?

University of California, Los Angeles, Professor Hal Hershfield conducted experiments on this very question. Using virtual reality, Hershfield had people interact with their future selves.

The results of his experiments revealed that people who interacted with their future selves were more likely to be concerned about both their present and future selves, and they also tended to act favorably in consideration of their future selves. For instance, they were much more likely to put money in a fake, experiment-based retirement account for the benefit of the future self they interacted with.

What did Hershfield's studies show us? The better we're able to visualize and interact with our future self, the better we get at taking good care of it. This is because by visualizing and connecting with our future self, we feel the reality of the upcoming circumstances and recognize how the actions of our present self are bound to create a real impact on our future self. We are faced with stark reminders that our actions aren't just taken in a vacuum and that most of them do have consequences.

By paying attention to our future selves, we start to see how a lack of self-discipline now may be good for our present self but disastrous for our future self. As we empathize with the fate of our future self and the kind of life it will have to live through if we keep our negative habits up (e.g., sleepless nights trying to get caught up with work, turning in haphazardly done output, having to deal with career failures), we begin to feel motivated to change our present ways to be *better*.

Other scientists have supported this notion. Research into chronic procrastination (perhaps the polar opposite of self-discipline) has unearthed an interesting discovery on what sets apart chronic procrastinators from the rest. For chronic procrastinators, that vision of their future selves tends to be blurry, more abstract, and impersonal.

They often feel an emotional disconnect between who they are at the present and who they'll become in the future. Rather than sacrifice present comfort for future rewards, they choose to revel in what feels good now because their vision tends to be more limited to the immediate moment. This is what psychology professor Dr. Fuschia Sirois calls *temporal myopia* (more easily thought of as nearsightedness with regards to time)—a key quality that also underlies a lack of self-discipline.

Thus, we find that simply closing the gap between your present and future self can bring perspective and force you into action. Imagine every little step and reaction your future self would make in both situations: where you falter and where you exercise your willpower. You already know which one will give your future self more pleasure, but really taste that pleasure. Chew on it and bring your full focus to it. As the allure and anticipation of that future pleasure grow larger, it begins to overshadow the pleasure of the present.

Now try to pig out at that all-you-can-eat buffet or use retail therapy in an attempt to fill your emotional needs. It just might become a little harder if you think about the consequences to yourself and think, "Oh, but I'll regret it tomorrow or next week…"

As you come to appreciate the beauty of that self-disciplined future, trace your way back from the future and right into the present day with your current decisions. It will be clear what you should be doing to reap the rewards and achieve that future.

A final way to travel through time is to think in terms of 10-10-10. The next time you feel you're about to lose your self-discipline and give in to your temptations, stop and try to transport yourself 10 minutes, 10 hours, and 10 days from the current moment. Why time intervals of 10 minutes, hours, and days? Because that helps you realize how short-term the pleasure or comfort of a discipline is relative to its long-term consequences.

At 10 minutes, you might be feeling good, with perhaps just the initial bit of shame creeping in. After 10 hours, you'll feel mostly shame or regret. Ten days later, you will inevitably be consumed by regret, having realized some of the negative consequences that your decision or action has had on your pursuit of your long-term goals. And for what? Likely no real benefit.

We usually know that we are doing something harmful in the moment, but that's not enough to stop us from doing it because we don't have any connection to our future self that will have to deal with the consequences. So disconnect from the emotional present by forcing yourself to think about a time when you are calm and unaffected—again, what would these future selves say? Would they be happy with your actions or ashamed, disapproving, and inconvenienced? Of course, this also has the nice benefit of inserting more time between your impulse and your actual decision, which always bodes well for you.

Suppose someone has just cut you off in traffic and almost caused you to crash. There was no damage done, but you are livid and on the verge of chasing them down in your car and assaulting them. You are seeing red. But now think about your future self in 10 minutes, hours, and days. Really try to live out those realities and thoroughly live out your emotional state in each of them.

In 10 minutes, you might be feeling pretty good still, filled with adrenaline and cortisol (triumph, self-adulation). In 10 hours, the reality will set in that you are being sued for millions of dollars (regret, embarrassment). In 10 days, you are arrested for felony assault (fear, anxiety, stress, shame). Nothing good here after the initial emotional catharsis.

For another example, imagine that you apply the 10-10-10 rule when deciding whether or not to skip a workout to go to dinner with coworkers. If you've just begun exercising and haven't built it into a consistent habit yet, your decision to skip a single workout might increase the odds of skipping future workouts or stopping working out altogether.

How will you feel in 10 minutes, hours, and days? Ten minutes—good, with a slight tinge of regret, as you can still taste the lasagna or ice cream. The pleasure is still tangible. Ten hours—almost entirely regret, as the pleasure is gone and fleeting and your diet has been soundly broken. Ten days—100% regret, because the broken discipline is now completely meaningless and but a faint memory. What was the point of it if you derive no benefit just 10 days later?

Remind yourself that you have a life to live beyond the current moment and that your current actions will either take you further away or closer to the life you want. There is an old Zen saying: "Your anger, depression, spite, or despair, so seemingly real and important right now; where will they have gone in a month, a week, or even a moment?"

Intense emotions blind us to the future and con us that now is all that matters. When we are incredibly angry or anxious, we can even forget that there is even going to *be* a future.

Behavior Chains

The next technique tricks the brain because it simulates that you actually don't have a choice to be disciplined or not. It's only when we come to a fork in the road that we have the ability to make a poor choice, so what if you minimize the number of forks in the road?

You can think of it as chaining behaviors together, but the technique itself is called the if-then technique. This is also sometimes known as an *implementation intention*—in other words, making your intention easy to implement. This is especially appropriate given that a lack of self-discipline is where good intentions go to die.

The *if* portion corresponds to the cue, while the *then* portion corresponds to the routine. If-then statements take the following form: if X happens, then I will do Y. That's it. This helps you exercise self-discipline because you never deal with it in the heat of the moment. You make the decision beforehand, when you are thinking more clearly and know what your best action will be. When actions are chained and given forethought, they tend to happen more often than not. They quickly become habitual, and you start to view them as inevitabilities rather than choices that you can avoid.

As a quick example, *if* it is 3:00 p.m. on Sunday, *then* you will call your mother. *If* it is 3:00 p.m., *then* you will drink two liters of water. *If* you have just taken a break, *then* you will take care of some chores. These are examples of when you use if-then to accomplish a specific goal—the first type of use. X can be whatever event, time, or occurrence you choose that happens on a daily basis, and Y is the specific action that you will take. It is perfect for ensuring that you exercise self-discipline and do what you're supposed to be doing.

The if-then statement simply takes your desired goals out of the ether and ties them to concrete moments in your day. A goal to eat healthier or get started on work has a set prescription because it is tied to a daily occurrence that is unavoidable. Instead of generalities, you get a time and place for when to act.

It seems simplistic, and it is, but it has been shown that you are two to three times more likely to succeed if you use an if-then plan than if you don't. In one study, 91% of people who used an if-then plan stuck to an exercise program versus 39% of non-planners. Peter Gollwitzer, the NYU psychologist who first articulated the power of if-then planning, recently reviewed results from 94 studies that used the technique and found significantly higher success rates for just about every goal you can think of, from using public transportation more frequently to avoiding stereotypical and prejudicial thoughts.

Let's say your significant other has been giving you a hard time about forgetting to text to inform them that you will be working late and not make dinner. For some, this requires self-discipline because it's something we must be aware of and can feel like a chore (sorry, everyone). So you make an if-then plan for this. It will sound like the following: if it is 6:00 p.m. and I'm at work, then I will text my significant other. Now the situation "6:00 p.m. at work" is wired in your brain directly to the action "text my sugar pie honeybunch."

Then the situation or cue "6:00 p.m. at work" becomes something your brain starts to fixate on. Below your conscious awareness, your brain starts scanning the environment, searching for the situation in the "if" part of your plan. Once the "if" part of your plan happens, the "then" part follows *automatically*. You don't *have* to consciously monitor your goal, which means your plans get carried out even when you are preoccupied.

The best part is that by detecting situations and directing behavior without conscious effort, if-then plans are far less taxing and require less willpower than mere resolutions. They enable us to conserve our self-discipline for when it's really needed and compensate for it when we don't have enough. Armed with if-thens, you can tell your fickle friend self-discipline that this year, you will be needing him less.

There's a second use for if-then plans, and it is also related to achieving a specific goal, but rather it's how to avoid *failing* at that goal. You would still use if X then Y, but X would be an unexpected situation that you want to maintain control in and deal with. In the first use, X is simply any everyday situation, occurrence, or event. Here, X is something that may not happen but you want to be prepared for. For instance, if you want to create a habit of drinking water, *if* you eat out at a restaurant, *then* you will get water with lemon only as opposed to soda or beer. That's a situation that isn't certain to occur, but it helps you adhere to your habit from the opposite end.

Complete these statements *before* you are in a dire situation and you can see how they work for you. It is like creating a rule for yourself to abide by. If you've given it thought beforehand, you can default to that guideline and not have to try to make a risky decision in the heat of the moment. Anticipate what's going to happen and you are a step ahead of the game. Again, this means that you make a self-disciplined choice before you are tempted and distracted with instant gratification.

Suppose it's your birthday, but you're on a strict diet and your office has a thing for surprise parties so you'll probably be getting one. "If they brought cake, then I'll turn it down and immediately drink a big glass of water." Alternatively, you could be having a problem with procrastination and you're settling in for a big project you have to finish. You could say, "If the phone rings, then I'll ignore it until I'm done."

"If I feel hungry, then I will order a salad instead of a hamburger."

"If I am shopping, then I will spend no more than $30."

You can get more detailed with these statements and can prepare them for situations with more significance or danger than the above examples. But whatever the case, the if-then method forces you to project yourself into common scenarios that could trigger reversion to your bad habits—

and makes you plan for those triggers. It takes away your residuals of false justification and excuses for doing the wrong thing (or doing nothing) and sharpens your commitment to meeting your goals.

Deciding exactly how you'll react to circumstances creates a link in your brain between the situation or cue (if) and the behavior that should follow (then). And as we know, everything good that we want happens in our brain; we just have to work around our brain's imperatives and tendencies to be a sloth and conserve as much energy as possible.

Pleasure Now, Pleasure Later

This next technique is all about addressing the pesky pleasure principle and how it tends to hijack our brains. It's also part of the reason we're stuck in the present and unable to think about future consequences or selves—we just want what we want, and we want it right now.

Luckily, there is a method to pair pleasure with a self-disciplined behavior that doesn't necessarily bear fruit until later in the future. It's called *temptation bundling*, and it aims to marry the needs of all versions of yourself.

Conceived by behavioral scientist Katy Milkman at the University of Pennsylvania, temptation bundling is a way to blend both future and present self needs by making future rewards more immediate. You give yourself instant gratification in the present while also achieving goals that benefit your future self in the long term. In our context, this is satisfying both the limbic system *and* the prefrontal cortex simultaneously.

It's simpler than it sounds.

If your goal is to satisfy the two versions of yourself (current and future), think about what that would require. Future self wants you to buckle down and take care of business so they are in a good position—or at least not suffering from your neglect. However, the current self wants to engage in hedonism and enjoy the present moment. Think eating Twinkies while working out, working out while watching TV, or doing work while soaking your feet in a salt bath—these are examples of ways to make the long term feel good at the present moment, and this is the essence of temptation bundling.

Bundle a temptation (current and immediate pleasure) with an unpleasurable activity (something you would otherwise procrastinate and that your future self would be pleased to avoid), and you get the best of both worlds.

There is no need to suffer in the present to get something done for your future self; if you do suffer, then you will lose all motivation and procrastinate. So find ways to bundle your temptations with your long-term goals. In other words, pair your obligations with instantaneous rewards.

Milkman found that up to 51% more of her study participants were willing to exercise with temptation bundling. Yes, you are strategically bribing yourself a little bit, but who ever said that self-discipline has to be 100% suffering? That's how you fail at it, while bundling the positive and negative together is how you trick the brain.

To use temptation bundling, you have to take an inventory of what you can use as pleasures/rewards. You already know the other part—what you are trying to avoid or must summon massive amounts of willpower to complete. You can make a list with two columns, one side being immediate pleasures for your present self and the other side being things you need to do for your future self. Then figure out creative ways to link the two conflicting columns in harmony.

Suppose you like chocolate, surfing, soccer, and running. But work, homework, and piano lessons stand in your way.

Chocolate	Homework
Surfing	Work
Soccer	Piano Lessons

How might you combine things to make the unpleasurable more tolerable? There are at least nine combinations of these elements and nine different ways you can bundle temptations. How might you combine chocolate with homework, soccer with work, and surfing with piano lessons? It doesn't take long to imagine how you can bribe yourself into doing exactly what you need to do. Hopefully, the temptation you seek doesn't directly undo the effects of your work, such as rewarding yourself with a donut for going to the gym, but sometimes it's worthwhile to take two steps forward and one step backward.

It's simple and can even work the opposite way in doling out small punishments in the absence of action—though that's not my particular cup of tea. That said, negativity does tend to be a more powerful motivating factor. For instance, you might pair a lack of finishing homework with a lack of chocolate or deprival of surfing the next day.

One thing to watch out for is the fact that humans quickly adapt to a certain level of stimulus, and it can take more and more of the same stimulus to achieve the same amount of motivation and pleasure. We build a tolerance, not unlike when we suddenly realize that we need 10 alcoholic drinks to feel tipsy after practicing for a whole summer. And thus, you should pay attention if your temptation bundling is waning in effect and you need to up the ante.

Overall, this technique can be used in combination with all the others so far, and it's aimed at keeping both of your selves and brains satisfied. You're not always in danger of burning out because you have something to work toward, and that provides a nice dopamine spike as well.

Speaking of dopamine...

Smaller, Faster, Closer

Self-discipline is often seen as a large boulder that you have to overcome with no respite. But what if we did three things to it, as the title of this section suggests: we broke it down into tiny components, we created the feeling that we were progressing and moving quickly, and then we also visualized how close we were to the finishing point.

Coincidentally, these three tactics create small, consistent spikes of dopamine to keep us engaged and chugging along toward our goals without even realizing it. We'll begin with breaking larger tasks down into tiny components.

When we're faced with huge tasks that feel insurmountable, it's such an obstacle that everything feels impossible and pointless. We drag our feet, discourage ourselves, and bitterly complain the whole time. More likely, we will just never get started, and our attempt at self-discipline will fail before it even begins.

For instance, a single huge task, such as "finish the two-hundred-page report," can certainly sound imposing, if not impossible. It's just so discouraging to try to get started on something like that because you feel that it will never end and you will never make any progress. To some extent, that's true, because even writing 10 pages is only completing 5% of the task. Imagine how hopeless you would feel.

However, what if you were to break that monumental task up into tiny, easy, individual tasks you could get to work on immediately, as well as see instant progress? For example: preparing the template, finding the first three sources, creating a bibliography, outlining five hundred words of the first section, and so on. Actually, it can go much smaller yet: choosing the fonts, writing the chapter titles, organizing the desk, formatting the document, or writing just one sentence. It can go even smaller still, but you can use your imagination for that.

The smaller, the better. When you break up the tasks that require self-discipline into as tiny pieces as possible, you are doing two things in particular.

First, as we've mentioned, you are making it easy to simply get started. The lower the boundary to entry, the better, and if you break your tasks down enough, you may not feel any resistance at all—for instance, turning on your computer and opening your word processing program. Second, you are providing a multitude of opportunities for dopamine spikes, because as you cross each little task off your list, you experience a sense of achievement and pleasure. This often becomes self-perpetuating and encourages you to keep going.

Anything difficult is only a series of easy things. Make your to-do list as long and articulated as possible, with as many small tasks as you can list. Instead of boulders, think in terms of pebbles—a pebble is something you can do instantly, without any effort and even with little thought.

Can you start a fire only with big logs? You might be able to, but it would be difficult. It's much more preferable to start with kindling, paper scraps, and small pieces of wood that burn easily. Small steps can take you to the top of the hill and let you roll down the other side to seize momentum.

They help you break the inertia that leads you to passivity and inaction.

Let's take an example that we're all familiar with: working out. You want to lose one hundred pounds, a hefty goal. If you go into the gym every day thinking that you want to lose one hundred pounds, you're going to fail. It's a huge, enormous boulder of a goal. It might sound grand to proclaim, but in reality, it is going to be very hard to stick to because of how unbelievable it sounds. In terms of daily actions, it's going to require an enormous lifestyle change, and that's nearly impossible to adhere to right out of the gate.

You won't see much progress on a daily or even weekly basis, and you will understandably become discouraged. What if you approach your weight loss goal by breaking it into small, manageable increments (goals) and tasks?

This might look something like setting a reasonable weekly weight loss goal, creating daily goals of eating specific foods (and not eating others), and drinking water every hour. Eat one hundred fewer calories per meal. Go on walks after each meal. Drink only half your soda. Eat five fewer fries each meal. Cook once a week. Buy the low-calorie version of snacks. Substitute water for fruit juice.

If you hit your weekly weight loss goal and successfully drink water every hour, it is far easier to stay motivated and focused. Meeting your smaller weekly goal will give you a sense of accomplishment (dopamine!), whereas making an insignificant dent in your total goal (one hundred pounds) will only make you feel discouraged and as if the task ahead is too great to achieve.

These are small tasks that, if done consistently and correctly, will lead to your overall goal of losing one hundred pounds. These tiny steps and frequent victories will encourage and motivate you to take action.

Does your first tiny step still feel like moving a boulder? One way to get the ball rolling no matter how you feel is to change your phrasing. "I'm going to finish that" turns into "I'm just going to get started on that." Just like with tiny steps, you make your threshold for starting as low as possible. In fact, you want to make it as low as possible so that it's nearly indistinguishable from the laziness of not acting at all.

Next, we move to how the feeling of *progress* also creates dopamine spikes and keeps us on track.

Remember that what is immediate is always more satisfying than something abstract and far off in the distant future. But we can trick our brains into thinking that far-off goals are actually more immediate than they are. By making our brains feel the constant churn of progress, we satisfy our emotional need for gratification in the present. Your immediate urges can be sated and your emotional brain kept happy, even though the actual fulfillment of the goal is still far off.

The progress principle is a little trick you can use to keep yourself motivated and on-task. Essentially, you want to be conducting any work toward a goal so that you can see the progress you're actually making, day by day, hour by hour. Record each period of work you achieve toward your goal. Rather than focusing on an uncompleted to-do list or some big goal far away in the future, you instead give yourself the opportunity to experience many smaller instances of progress. Anything you can do that brings your self-disciplined behavior and ties it to what is actually being achieved helps, otherwise you can feel like you are just acting for acting's sake.

What could be more motivating? Harvard professor Teresa Amabile popularized this concept with her research. She analyzed work diaries of knowledge workers and was fascinated by how people structured their perceptions during a workday.

The study asked 238 people in different organizations to keep daily experience diaries. The researchers analyzed over

12,000 separate entries on these people's inner perceptions, motivation at work, emotions, and performance levels. It was found that the biggest factor behind motivation and positive emotion at work was feeling as though one was making progress toward a meaningful goal. People who consistently took small steps toward meaningful projects ended up being more productive, creative, and engaged with their work. They also had better work relationships and overall better performance. Recognizing and celebrating little achievements in service of a large achievement kept people on track, in other words.

Of course, experiencing the end result of a completed goal is marvelous, but it seems to be all the more powerful when broken into smaller, more readily available chunks in the present. Amabile found that the more frequently people gave themselves the opportunity to experience progress, the higher quality their work overall, the better their performance, and the greater their satisfaction.

There are endless ways to make your progress feel more current and tangible: write down your achievements and small milestones. Give yourself credit for completing hourly or half-hourly chunks. Thus, motivation and reward work in tandem to keep you on track and focused. Without pausing to tally up how much you've already done, the mind can come to believe that no achievement has been made—after all, the major end goal feels just as distant as it did at the start of the workday.

The progress principle biases your experience toward the present and gives your emotional brain something to celebrate. That means it's less likely to sabotage you later on with doubts, fears, laziness, or procrastination.

Remember, "what gets rewarded gets repeated." The behavior you take the time to become aware of and encourage is more likely to happen in the future. So using the progress principle is one way to train your brain into a positive feedback loop, working consistently toward your goal rather than resisting it or procrastinating. Teach yourself to associate self-discipline with reward.

The focus is always, however, on the process. An end result is never guaranteed, but we have a lot more control over the everyday processes right now. Whatever happens, you can look at your work at the end of the day and know that you've achieved. Turn toward progress and not outcome, and you engage yourself in the present and give yourself a chance to notice and reward hard work, even if it's hard work that may seem minuscule in the grand scheme of things.

As you figure out how to use this principle yourself, remember to mark your progress in as tangible of a way as possible. Make sure you're not only visually seeing your progress, but take the time to stop and actually *feel* that progress. Let those feelings of achievement and satisfaction sink in. It's this emotional component (and the corresponding dopamine hit in the brain!) of achievement that will keep you motivated, focused, and performing well.

You can do the classic technique of writing a to-do list and watch as you cross things off as the day progresses. Or you can make a chart that you actively color in or tear strips off of. If you're trying to reach a savings goal, use a clear jar to collect a penny for every $10 you save. The ritual of placing the pennies inside every day will give you a deep sense of satisfaction and movement toward your goal. Consider pausing at the end of every day to record and tally up the hours spent on working toward goals and the small milestones you've achieved. Actively tell yourself, "I'm closer to achieving my goal," and appreciate the feeling and associated dopamine hit.

Finally, let's talk about the last way that we can trick our brains—the feeling that you are close to your end goal, even if you aren't necessarily. This is known as the *goal gradient hypothesis*. Behaviorist Clark L. Hull was the first to express this principle. Hull determined that human beings are much more motivated to reach their goals if they are closer to their completion.

A series of studies published in the *Journal of Marketing Research* bore this truth out. One study observed people taking part in a very common coffee shop reward plan, where you receive one free espresso drink after you buy a certain number of them (usually 10, from my experience). It's that plan where the café tracks your purchases on a card, which they stamp every time you buy a drink. After you get 10 stamps, you get your freebie.

In the beginning of the cycle—say, the first five or so—customers took more time between purchases. But the closer they got to that free beverage, the more frequently they came to buy coffee. The researchers found that, over the course of the 10-drink cycle, the time between coffee purchases decreased by about 20% at each step. Their motivation and taste of completion grew the closer they got to the completion of a goal, no matter how insignificant.

Furthermore, if the customers saw visible cues representing their goal, they moved even faster. Some customers got cards with two preexisting "bonus" stamps at the end of their 10-drink purchase; others just got cards showing the 10 purchase stamps with no spaces for the pending free drinks. Those who had cards with the pre-filled bonus stamps completed their 10-drink purchases faster than those who didn't—in terms of average rate and speed, not just because they had a two-stamp head start.

Another study in the same series involved visitors to a music-rating website. The site initiated a rewards program in which users received a $25 online gift certificate once they rated 51 different songs. Each song contained about 50 different rating scales that the user used to judge the music—for example, if the music was more peaceful or aggressive, more mellow or upbeat, and more sad or happy. The average user spent four minutes rating each song—not an eternity, but not a quickie either.

Some visitors finished all 51 songs in one visit, and some failed to meet that goal at all. The remaining participants, who completed the program in two or more visits, exhibited results that echoed the coffee shop rewards card experiment: the closer they got to their goal, the longer they stayed on the site and the more rapidly they went through their song ratings. The tangible feeling of progress and motion were motivating in their own right, perhaps even more so than the task or rewards themselves.

In both the coffee and song-rating trials, once the participants reached their goals and received their free rewards, they "reset" and slowed down their participation in each program. The attainment of the goal and receipt of the reward brought their engagement back down to early-stage levels.

The goal gradient hypothesis holds true even when one is offered a greater reward at a later time. For example, if the song-raters above were offered a $200 gift certificate after rating 408 songs, most wouldn't have been quite as motivated at the beginning stages as they were when the deal was $25 after 51 ratings. The incremental offering of rewards worked better because they'd get their prize much sooner, even if the payoff was smaller. The earlier the award is given out, the more motivated people will be to act.

This behavior has strong implications for how we might approach increasing self-discipline and adherence to our best intentions. The primary finding is that people are motivated by things that are *coming up soon*. If those free coffees came after seven purchases rather than 10, chances are the customers would flood the café.

It's just a matter of "moving the goalposts." We know that people are motivated by progress, ticking off boxes, and getting closer to any arbitrary finish line. So instead of focusing on a huge goal that's far away, try establishing a series of goalposts with smaller incentives so you can harness that feeling on a consistent, frequent basis. Track as many steps as possible to be able to feel the progress and feel a constant sense of motion.

For example, instead of focusing on losing 40 pounds in eight months, you might set a goal of losing 10 pounds in two months. It may have also been a good idea to stagger the goal amounts as time progressed: five pounds in the first month, six pounds in the second, seven pounds in the third, and so on.

To feel surer about his efforts, he might track his efforts between each smaller goal: how many miles he completes on the treadmill, how many reps he does on each step of the circuits, his daily caloric intake. Keeping himself aware of how much progress he's making on a daily basis toward a smaller goal will make him more motivated to gradually increase his efforts.

Moving the goalposts also lessens the probability that you'll procrastinate. It's tough to get worked up for a grander goal that's a long way off when there is no sense of impact from any of your actions. If a writer gives themselves a goal of finishing a 135,000-word book in six months, they may feel that 500 words here or there will make no difference to such a huge sum, and thus they won't work for the day. Or they might even figure that the number is too lofty and put off starting.

But taking the cue from the goal gradient hypothesis, what if the writer were to break things down into finishing 6,000 words in a week—or even 750 words in a day? What about 375 words in the morning and 375 words at night? That's almost unavoidable. You'd really have to *try* to not meet that if you were a professional writer. It's much easier to visualize and to accomplish right now, so chances are, that writer would be more willing to start chasing that goal immediately. Again, it's about a sense of constant motion and progress. The converse—standing still or even stagnating—is decidedly *not* motivating.

Finally, having more frequent, slightly smaller goals also does wonders for our sense of personal achievement. If we're meeting multiple short-term goals over a certain period of time, we're giving ourselves more positive reinforcement more often. We're continually giving ourselves affirmation that we can accomplish things.

One of the biggest hurdles to self-discipline is looking at tasks as huge, inseparable boulders. It's intimidating and discouraging, and when those emotions arise, it's tough to avoid procrastinating because tackling a boulder is a tough sell. Unfortunately, this is a habit that plagues most people. They see only massive boulders and allow themselves to get emotionally thrown off track.

Meeting more recurrent, lesser goals more often sends our psyche a positive message. And the closer we get to the goal (while also breaking it down into tiny sub-goals and harnessing the feeling of progress), the more quickly we'll work to finish it. This constant reaffirmation and reassurance help us break the cycle of apathy.

Takeaways:

- It turns out that we need to trick the brain and work with it instead of directly battling its natural tendencies

and trying to change them. Good luck with that! We need to treat the brain like an angry and grumpy infant—you can't just tell it to stop crying; you need to be strategic.
- The first strategy to trick our brains into self-discipline is to proactively consider tomorrow—in other words, your future self and how today's decisions will impact him or her. We are usually too stuck in only the present, but just like we have two brains, we have two selves we should keep in mind. So imagine and visualize your future self's life when you are faltering or struggling with a decision. It will help keep you focused on what needs to be done for your ultimate happiness.
- Behavior chains, or if-then statements, or implementation intentions, are another method to tricking the brain. They work because they remove the choice from your hands, and thus self-disciplined behavior is almost the expectation. It works simply as "if X, then Y," where X is an everyday occurrence and Y is your desired action.

The more concrete you make your intentions, the more likely they are to happen.
- Temptation bundling tricks the brain because it gives the brain the dopamine and pleasure it seeks but ties it to a self-disciplined act. Yes, this is using carrots as motivators or simply bribing yourself to set yourself into motion and stay on track. It's as easy as it sounds.
- As the brain wants pleasure as soon as possible, there are a few ways we can simulate that feeling. First is to break your desired tasks or behaviors into the smallest components possible. This allows you to reduce the barrier to getting started and also feel a constant sense of victory. Second, we can keep track of all victories and notice how much progress is constantly being made. Third, we will also feel more motivated and disciplined if we sense that we are relatively close to completion.

Chapter 3. Trick the Brain Pt. 2

Our brains are so sneaky at self-preservation and energy conservation that these things usually occur without our conscious awareness.

At this point, we should remember *the imperatives of the brain (that we must defeat)* from the prior chapter:

- The brain is locked in an epic battle with itself, between the instinct for the quickest reaction (emotion) and the most optimal reaction (logic).
- The brain wants as much pleasure as possible, as fast as possible; an absence of pain and discomfort will also do in most cases.

- Speed is of the essence for the brain.
- The brain never wants to sacrifice anything pleasurable.

It's pretty easy to see how these biological intentions can be constantly running in the background. Just think about the immediate and powerful impulses that rush into your head when you walk by a fragrant bakery. If you're hungry, you might be overtaken by this opportunity to satisfy one of your most primal urges.

And again, that's what we are trying to fight with neuro-discipline. You could say that it's a losing battle, but there are more techniques and approaches we can use to avoid directly fighting our instincts (no dopamine, no pleasure, no enjoyment!) and instead work around them.

Deconstruct Pleasure

We were introduced to the pleasure principle in the first chapter, and we've mentioned it here and there ever since. But we haven't directly talked about how to make the pleasure principle work for you instead of treating it like something that simply sabotages you. We take a deeper look at the pleasure principle in this section and deconstruct what we can actually categorize as pleasure itself.

Remember that the pleasure principle theoretically dictates everything we do. More is better, and faster is even more important. And we can make this work for us if we analyze what we consider as pleasure (and pain). We can crank up pains and pleasures in ways that benefit us psychologically and keep us thinking in a disciplined manner. Writer Guillermo Rubio provided a list of steps on how you can do this.

1. Decide what you want. What is your ultimate ambition or goal—even the one that seems wholly improbable or unlikely but you really have a desire to achieve?

Shoot for the stars here, regardless of your current circumstances. Maybe you're a recent high school graduate who dreams of going to medical school and becoming a neurosurgeon. Or maybe you're an entry-level office worker who dreams of starting a video production company. Or you're a middle-aged manager who wants to retire to the south of France. Or maybe you're a karaoke host who wants to become the world's most beloved entertainer.

Don't limit yourself. Allow yourself to dream about what you most want to accomplish in life. If your idea sounds crazy or impossible, that's even better. This is the ultimate long-term pleasure that keeps you in motion when you want to give up. This is what you would be sacrificing if you quit.

2. Take inventory of your pain and pleasure. This is where you take aspects of the pleasure principle and start working them to your benefit. Here's what you do:

- Take two sheets of paper. Draw a line down the middle of each page.

- At the top of the left column on both pages, write down "PAIN AVOIDED."

- At the top of the right column on both pages, write down "PLEASURE GAINED."

- Now, at the top-center of one of the pages, write down "TAKING ACTION."

- At the top-center of the other pages, write down "NOT TAKING ACTION."

By now you probably know what we're up to. You're going to list the pain and pleasure you expect you'll experience when you take a step toward accomplishing your goal or when you decide not to. To motivate yourself psychologically, you're going to amp up the pain associated with not taking action and the pleasure associated with taking action. This may seem elementary, but it's a level of perspective and insight that you can use to combat your impulses.

For example, let's take that dream of quitting a job and working to start a video production company. Let's go with the "NOT TAKING ACTION" bit first. Remember, we want to amp up the pain associated with a lack of self-discipline. It might look something like this:

NOT TAKING ACTION to start video production company	
PAIN AVOIDED	PLEASURE GAINED
Risk of financial hit	Maintaining financial security
Hassle of starting a business from scratch	Continuing in job I'm comfortable with
Disruption of current life	Peace of mind with family

That's a fairly compelling list. Now let's make one up for "TAKING ACTION":

TAKING ACTION to start video production company	
PAIN AVOIDED	PLEASURE GAINED
Feeling like a personal failure	Financial independence
Feeling trapped working for someone else	Artistic accomplishment
Feeling personally unfulfilled	Satisfaction with career

List as many pain and pleasure points as you can for each scenario. Be honest with yourself and try to think the potential through as much as you can. You should get some clarity about what your aspirations and ambitions are—not to mention your hopes and fears.

3. Tip the scales in your favor. This is a part where you get creative and build up your emotional resolve. Take the "NOT TAKING ACTION" sheet you've made up and go through the pain and pleasure points. Then make statements or rationalizations that would make *not* acting more painful. Tip the scales in your favor, so to speak, to allow the negative bias of our minds to motivate you. Understand exactly what pains await you and really amplify them. For example, in our video production company:

- You might mitigate the "Disruption of current life" pain point by saying, "But after a few years in business, I would make my current life better."

- For the pleasure point of "Continuing in job I'm comfortable with," you might add, "But being miserable about never having taken the chance to break from it."

- For the pleasure point of "Peace of mind with family," you might say, "But if I'm miserable about not having taken a chance, my family's not going to feel positive anyway, so how can that be peace of mind?"

Do this for every entry on your "NOT TAKING ACTION" list. Hopefully a sense of just how lousy this option is will emerge.

4. Visualize the positive effects of taking action. Now go to your "TAKING ACTION" list and revisit each item you've listed. This time do the exact opposite of the other sheet: picture how utterly fantastic each of these situations could turn out. Think about the best-case scenarios that could result with each of these items if you go for it:

- For the pain point of "Feeling trapped working for someone else," visualize being the person in charge at your own company. Imagine how it will feel not to answer to somebody other than your clients. Think about how you'll have the freedom to set up your business however you like. Picture that sweet corner office with a view.

- For the pleasure point of "Artistic accomplishment," think about the projects you'd take on. Imagine working with creative people and the kind of work you'd produce. Go ahead and get fanciful and picture winning an Emmy.

- For the pleasure point of "Financial independence," think about what you might do with all the money you keep for yourself. Maybe you'll be able to get out of debt. You might take an overseas vacation you've been wanting to take for years. You might buy a house. You might buy a boat. A boat with bedrooms and a full kitchen.

Again, go all out with Step 4. Take the positive possibilities and run with them. Don't be surprised if you get a minor dopamine rush just from this action alone.

This sheet is more than just an inventory: it's a checklist for reinforcing your self-discipline in a way that our brains will understand. Each line should serve as a little trigger that has a positive impact on your will to achieve what you want. This is a classic instance of not necessarily fighting our brain's tendencies; we are still giving it what it wants, just in a way that suits our long-term thinking.

Environmental Assistance

One of the biggest influencers of self-discipline is the environment in which you're implementing it. Environmental factors can either enable discipline or weaken it, and it's unlikely that they will play no role at all. They can trigger our brain's worst tendencies or lull them to sleep like an innocent baby.

Designing and maintaining an environment that's conducive to self-discipline is one of the simplest ways to trick the brain. The best environments are ones that you don't need to rely on self-discipline. If you design it correctly, you can set yourself up for success because your desired action or outcome will occur naturally. This tricks the brain by keeping its instincts out of sight and out of mind.

An underrated part about self-discipline is about not having to exercise it at all, removing the distractions and temptations. We all understand this when it's obvious—you wouldn't go into an Italian restaurant known for its homemade pasta if you're trying to avoid carbs, for example. You're bound to have more success with losing weight if you live in a gym versus living in an ice cream factory. But there may be some less obvious ways that you can improve the ways that environmental factors are influencing your self-discipline.

First of all, your environment really doesn't need to include temptations or distractions.

Stanford Graduate School of Business Professor Baba Shiv conducted a study that illustrated the effect of distractions. Shiv distracted one group of participants by asking them to remember a phone number and then asked all the study participants to choose either chocolate cake or fruit. Those who were trying to remember phone numbers chose the cake 50% more often than those who weren't. The conclusion here is that focus is an essential part of being disciplined.

If you're constantly distracted, you succumb to temptations without even giving yourself a chance to exercise your self-discipline. It just doesn't occur to you, and you choose the path of least resistance despite your best intentions. You lose awareness of your actions and default to the pleasure principle's influence. This process can sneakily go on in the background so that we don't even realize that our discipline is lapsing until it's too late and all of our past efforts have been wasted.

The design of checkout lanes in supermarkets is a prime example of capitalizing on distracted minds. You can make healthy decisions every step of the way through the grocery store, but you can't escape without one final distraction of candy, chocolate, and snacks at the register. This is frequently the most difficult time to be disciplined because you're so close to exiting and thinking ahead and the items are cheap and available to purchase instantly.

If you work in a cluttered environment, clean it up. A clean desk can help create a clear mind, and a clear mind is much more able to remain self-disciplined. A Cornell University study provides some compelling evidence supporting the concept of *"out of sight, out of mind"* as a means of improving discipline, and it applies to far more beyond your desk.

The study participants were given a jar full of Hershey's Kisses that was either clear or opaque and either placed on their desk or six feet away. On average, the participants ate 7.7 Kisses per day from the clear jars on their desks as opposed to 4.6 per day from opaque jars in the same location. When the jars were placed six feet away, the participants ate 5.6 Kisses per day from the clear jars and 3.1 per day from the opaque jars.

Surprisingly, the study subjects consistently reported feeling that they had eaten more Kisses when the jars were placed six feet away, even though the opposite was true. That discrepancy is a crucial piece of information because it provides a simple guideline for improving discipline. That is, you can use laziness to your advantage by clearing your workplace of distractions. You may not completely forget about those distractions, but the more effort it takes for you to give in to a temptation, the less likely you are to do so. Furthermore, it eliminates some of the most counterproductive discipline lapses—the mindless ones that we don't even realize we are doing.

It's so much easier to reach your hand into a cookie jar without thinking about it if that jar is easily accessible and visible. Those are the types of scenarios that you want to avoid when designing an environment for discipline. If you place the cookie jar in a distant cabinet, you don't eliminate the temptation altogether, but you make it so that giving in to the temptation requires a lot of effort. That makes a big difference.

Ultimately, you want to create an environment for yourself that is clear of distractions and obvious temptations. You can make discipline drastically easier just by eliminating the mindless and effortless lapses in discipline that are made possible by an environment that hasn't been optimized.

Optimizing your environment for self-discipline really comes down to understanding how automatic most of your decision-making is.

To illustrate that point, consider the findings of a study conducted in 11 European countries on organ donors. The data showed that countries that automatically have citizens opted-in to being organ donors—requiring action to opt-out—had rates at or above 95% participation. When the default choice was not to be an organ donor, however, the highest rate found in any of the 11 countries was a mere 27% participation. Ultimately, people just went with the option that required the least effort. It said nothing about their actual intention or desire to be an organ donor.

This same concept of defaulting to the more desirable choice can be applied to your own self-discipline. We're lazy and will happily accept whatever is in front of our faces. Most of the time, this is detrimental. You can make it easy for yourself to choose whichever options most benefit you while also making it as difficult as possible to make harmful decisions.

A default option is one that the decision-maker chooses if he or she does nothing or the minimal amount of effort. In other contexts, default options also include those that are normative or suggested. Countless experiments and observational studies have shown that making an option the default will increase the likelihood of it being chosen, which is known as the default effect. Making decisions requires energy, so we often choose the default option to conserve energy and avoid making decisions, especially when we aren't familiar with what it is we are making a decision about.

Optimizing these default decisions is where the bulk of your efforts to make a more discipline-conducive environment can take place. You might believe that you control the majority of your choices, but in reality, that isn't the case. Instead, many of your actions are just responses to your environment. It really begins with the process of diagnosing what you are in the habit of mindlessly being distracted by and then removing them. Make it difficult to *not* do something you're supposed to or to do something you're supposed to.

If you're distracted by social media, for example, you might move the app icons to the back page of your phone so that you aren't constantly seeing them whenever you open your phone to do something else. Better yet, you can log out of the apps after each use or delete them from your phone altogether so that you'll only use them when you really want to instead of letting them be distractions.

And if you're in the habit of mindlessly picking up your phone while working, you can simply start placing it faced down and far enough away that you have to get up to reach it. If you want to practice violin more, put it on your desk with your music notes open. If you want to floss your teeth more, keep floss in your backpack, in your bathroom, on your nightstand, and on your sofa.

There is a seemingly endless number of examples of how you can utilize the default effect to become more disciplined with very little use of willpower itself. Another one is that leaving potato chips and cookies out on the kitchen counter will make it your default choice to eat those things whenever you walk to the kitchen and are feeling even the slightest bit hungry. Hiding those (or not buying them at all) and replacing those unhealthy snacks with fruit will instantly increase the probability that you eat fruit and that you avoid the unhealthy snacks. Want to exercise more? Put a pull-up bar in your bathroom doorway.

If you keep sugary sodas and juices in your refrigerator, you're making it your default choice to drink them whenever you are thirsty and open the fridge. But if you don't have those options, you increase the likelihood that you'll drink water or make tea. Want to take more vitamins? Put them right next to your toothbrush for easier access.

If you sit in an office all day and have back problems, then you might benefit from standing up and walking frequently throughout the day. You can make this your default option by drinking water constantly so that you are forced to get up to go to the bathroom. Or perhaps you could schedule alarms on your phone and place it somewhere out of reach so that you have to stand up to turn off the alarm whenever it goes off.

The whole point of this is that you can save your energy by making positive changes to your environment. The two biggest facets of environmental change are reducing clutter and distractions and optimizing choices based on the default effect. These all make it so you can sidestep actually using self-discipline and save it for your bigger daily challenges. After all, why exercise willpower when you don't need to if you can plan around it?

Something that we've been dancing around is the concept of saving your self-discipline or willpower and generally conserving your energy. Why is this so important?

It turns out that our brains have a limited number of decisions we can meaningfully analyze and make, and the more decisions we look at, the more fatigued we get. The prefrontal cortex is like our calf muscle that grows tired and eventually stops working in the correct way. At that point, you're likely to break your self-discipline no matter how hard you try. This is a phenomenon more generally known as *ego depletion*, and it applies exactly the same way in regard to discipline.

Ego depletion is the idea that our mental resources for specific activities are limited. When the resources drain or are decreased, those specific mental activities perform poorly. It was first discovered in relation to self-control, where experiments (Baumeister et al., 1998) showed that subjects who resisted chocolate performed worse and gave up earlier on a puzzle task. In other words, ego depletion was in full effect, and the amount of self-control they exhibited in resisting the chocolate directly weakened their ability to persist with the puzzle task.

Self-discipline and decision quality decreased quickly as ego depletion started to take place. If you're thinking that you've read something recently that claims that ego depletion has come into doubt in recent years, that's true, and we'll discuss that at the end of this section.

Once you get over the initial surprise that something as small as making a self-disciplined decision can deplete your mental resources, you begin to find that it makes all too much sense. The brain requires energy to act and think. In fact, the brain requires up to 20% of our daily energy consumption, despite being only 2% of the mass of our bodies. It works hard, and the act of discipline is not something that's easy.

The thought process involved in the debate of overindulging in chocolate or not can be quite lengthy, and as the experiment showed, it can eliminate your capacity for self-control and discipline in the future. It's easy to resist chocolate once or twice, but when you encounter the temptation repeatedly throughout the day, your self-control will likely erode, and it will become nearly impossible to say no—because your brain will run out of juice to do so.

Further support for the theory of ego depletion came in the form of feeding versus starving the brain and then seeing what happened while using self-control.

Experiments showed that using self-control depleted the brain of glucose, its primary energy source, and that ingesting sources of nutrition and glucose could reverse ego depletion and energize people's sense of discipline and self-control. Self-control uses a significant amount of your brain's power reserves, and purely exercising self-control can make you function noticeably lower overall.

Once again, discipline is not an endless quantity, and we must recognize the underlying biological basis just like with energy in general. Our capacity for self-discipline can be easily drained, so the question is how to safeguard this reservoir of brainpower to use when you need it. How can you keep yourself primed for big pushes of self-discipline as often as possible or when you know you'll need it?

Start by viewing your self-discipline as a battery that only has so much charge. How would you protect your smartphone's battery if you knew that you were going to be watching three hours of video on it later? Decision-making, motivating, and using self-control all draw from the same pool of the prefrontal cortex, so these are the activities you need to be mindful of.

You should try to get a sense of what is trivial in your day in terms of motivation, decisions, or self-discipline—and remove or avoid them.

How do you know if it's trivial? If it's truly trivial, it won't matter if you ignore it, or the choices you make will have no ill effect that lasts longer than a few minutes. This is a tough step for most of us because we are trained to give our full and undivided attention to something, lest we perform it poorly. In a way, this point advocates simply seeing what you can get away with paying little attention to—for your prefrontal cortex's sake. Every percentage of your battery you save for that task later makes a difference.

Trivial decisions should only be allocated a trivial amount of mental bandwidth, so just try to keep things proportional so you can preserve as much as possible for when you need it. If something doesn't impact your life, take it off your plate as soon as possible.

The overall aim of this point is to make fewer conscious choices per day. Instead of even dealing with some decisions, you could also choose to automate them—in other words, pick only one option and stick with it for consistency and ease. In a sense, you are making rules for yourself to ignore your choices and stick with—for instance, one lunch, one outfit, one music playlist, and one method of doing things. Of course, this is entirely tied into our environments and setting ourselves up for success.

This is also the purported reason famous Apple founder Steve Jobs had a standard uniform of sneakers, a black turtleneck, and comfortable jeans. It was so he could avoid making decisions and save his brainpower for when he actually needed it. On a daily basis, this can truly transform into energy you can use for maximum discipline and motivation.

Your mental resources always recharge, but they are easily depleted. Get into battle mode and treat your brain like a muscle that you need for peak self-discipline.

As mentioned earlier, there has been doubt cast on ego depletion in recent years as a scientific theory. Some follow-up studies have found inconclusive results based on Baumeister's work, and others have found that ego depletion was only found when the participants already knew about the theory prior to being studied—it gives people an easy excuse to give up on things, as a result of "being drained."

Ego depletion may not be conclusively proven, but we can still make a credible argument that consciously having to think about 10 tasks in a day is more mentally strenuous than thinking about two tasks in a day. The more you have to think about, the less self-discipline you will be able to muster up. The argument for lessening the load on the prefrontal cortex remains the same; the term just changes slightly from ego depletion to overall energy depletion.

Shift Your Focus

Finally, we come to the concept of shifting your focus for self-discipline. We all have big goals for our lives. Every one of us is acting, consciously or unconsciously, toward some endpoint or specific result—and life would feel meaningless if we didn't do so.

But the trouble with goals is they shift our focus into a realm we actually don't have much control over: the future. When we are forward-focused and looking at some distant outcome, we disconnect from the present. And the present is the only place where we have any control over whether that outcome gets created or not.

A key element of better self-discipline is the counterintuitive practice of deliberately turning to the small, everyday processes that eventually cumulate in the end goal, rather than the end goal itself. As an example, many people who struggle with their weight might set a goal for themselves to reach a certain goal weight. They focus on the endpoint, the moment when they've achieved that outcome and are already at the size they want to be. They think, "Yes, *this* is what I want," and commit to that goal. What could be more natural?

However, actually achieving that goal is something that takes place quietly, bit by bit, action by action, in each passing moment. The person in our example might wholeheartedly commit to what they think of as the goal—enjoying the achievement of completion at the end—so that when day-to-day reality appears, their commitment flies out the window. When faced with temptation or procrastination, they buckle and forget all about the grand finish line at the end.

This is because, although goals *finish* in the future, they're built right here, in the present. The workshop for each little part of our desired outcome is the ordinary choices and experiences in each passing moment. To be disciplined is to respect that it is your daily behaviors, cumulatively, that result in the grand finale. You cannot focus on the grand finale alone.

This is a simple idea: focus on process rather than outcome. There's a good reason to shift your perspective and focus on the small-scale. Once you can reliably perform your daily tasks toward your goal, day in and day out, the desired outcome will naturally follow. It's the old "take care of the cents and the dollars will follow" principle.

Yes, we should absolutely set goals, and we should absolutely be aware of precisely what those goals are. But to bring those goals to life, we need to zoom in again and get to the business of ticking off those smaller tasks, one at a time, day after day. When we can do this consistently and with good effort, the results take care of themselves.

Thinking this way empowers you since you actually don't have control over the big, overwhelming goal somewhere far off in the imagined distance. But you *do* have control over what you do right now, in this moment. You can decide to put in the hours today, tomorrow, and the day after that. This is the proper place to focus your activities—not in some as-yet unreal future moment.

The thing about goals is that they are abstract. They're not actually *real*, at least not until you bring them to life with concrete action. And more than that, it's not a single concrete action that brings your dream to life, but a consistent, ongoing series of regular actions (i.e., a habit). It's easy to look at some faraway goal and think it would be nice to be there. But until you can commit to a real change in habit to help you cover the distance between you and that goal, the goal means absolutely nothing.

The goal is the *what* but to get there, you'll need a *how*.

The little things in life are easy to ignore because they're so, well, little. What does an hour here or there matter? Is a missed workout such a big deal? The thing is, the little things tend to add up to big things. In fact, your life right now is nothing more than the sum total of all the many millions of little things that have passed you by so far. The trick is that these little things add up whether you're conscious of them or not. You can choose to let those opportunities float by, using each moment to cement useless behaviors, or you can use each tiny moment to gradually build toward a future you care about.

Isn't it amazing how people find it so easy to say, "Yes of course I want to lose 100 pounds!" but immediately become hesitant when put on the spot to lose just one pound over the next week? The small things, in other words, are big things. Goals are cheap—what matters is *consistent action* taken toward them.

So try to avoid focusing on the outcome and simply hoping that the corresponding behavior will follow. When you focus on the endpoint, what you do is forget about the details of how you're going to get there. You forget that you're going to have to do a ton of hard work, over and over again. You forget, in other words, all those smaller in-between stages when you're not yet at your goal but still on the way.

So as in our example, you may do a diet and exercise program for a month, then get on the scale and be dismayed when you're nowhere near your goal yet. You feel like you failed because you haven't achieved your goal when you would have been better off acknowledging the amazing habits that you had maintained for a whole month. Challenges and pressures mount, and you give up. You were looking out over the horizon instead of at your feet, and you stumbled.

There's another way to do this though. Being process-oriented means you reward yourself for following through with behavior you know is conducive to reaching your goal. You don't wake up every day with an enormous goal hanging over your head. You wake up knowing that today you have only one job: to do those behaviors that will lead to your goal. So you eat right, head to the gym, and skip dessert. You get on the scale after a month and see a modest weight loss and celebrate. You're on the right path! You recognize that every day for a full month you committed to conscious, beneficial action in the right direction. You feel good about yourself, "bank" your gains emotionally, and feel inspired to keep going. You can't wait to see what another month of effort will achieve.

Can you see the difference? In both of these examples, the end goal is no less relevant. It's just that in one, the real nuts and bolts of the *process* are the focus. In the former, feeling the huge distance between where you're at and the endpoint is enough to get discouraged and revert to old behaviors. Focusing on the goal only makes you painfully aware of how you haven't reached it yet. But when you focus on processes, every day that you can stick to your new habit is a cause for celebration. Every day you give yourself the chance to strengthen your self-discipline.

Don't let the perfect be the enemy of the good. Don't let the big picture make you forget about all the little things the big picture is made of. Focus on what you can control, not in an abstract, "one day" sort of way, but right now, every day.

Self-discipline is the attitude we take to our day-to-day tasks in service of the bigger goal we care about. It's the *how*. It's the process of routinely turning our awareness and actions away from distraction and instant gratification and toward building our dreams, one piece at a time. Sacrifice, hard work, resilience—all these are part of self-discipline, and every one of them takes place right here, in the present moment. Self-discipline is a habit, not an outcome. It's a code of conduct you adopt *permanently*.

This could mean routinely pushing yourself to stop procrastinating and put in an hour of piano practice, day in and day out. It could mean consistently telling yourself that you will not have a cigarette, no matter how badly you want one. It could mean developing the habit of waking up early, every single day, no excuses.

The great news about all this effort is that even if they don't actually land you the goal you want, you still benefit. In time, you may start to see discreet, measurable goals as less valuable to you than consistent behavior you can master over a lifetime. After all, which sounds better: losing a few extra pounds or maintaining a healthy diet and lifestyle for the rest of your life?

Again, taking care of the small stuff means you don't have to worry so much about the big stuff. When you can focus on consistent, healthy behaviors that create a meaningful, self-disciplined life, it's hard to think of any goal or outcome that isn't more available to you as a result.

When we look at goals, it's easy to imagine them as immense mountains we have to climb to the top. In reality, there is no mountain. You have to build it. And you can only do that bit by bit.

Step 1: What is your ideal self?

Your ideal self is the best, most evolved version of you. Your experiences, your relationships, your occupation, your possessions. What is your life all about? Imagine this person in as much detail as you can.

Now, take this version of yourself and imagine what life would be if you were this person in 10 days' time. Picture it concretely. Fast-forward and imagine the same thing but in 10 weeks from now. Then 10 months from now. Then 10 years. You get the picture. This is the "mountain" (i.e., your goal).

Step 2: What habits are associated with this ideal self?

Now comes the work. What behaviors and practices go with this ideal self you've envisioned? In order to be this person that you've imagined, what actions must you take to actually live that life?

Maybe you decide that your ideal self is fit and healthy. When you picture this person in your mind's eye, you see that they exercise daily. You also see that they read an hour every night before bed and never drink alcohol. You see that they take time every day to connect with their spouse and spend time outdoors. These are not goals anymore, but daily disciplines your ideal self naturally partakes in.

Step 3: Break these disciplines into tiny habits.

Let's look closer at each of these. To exercise daily, your ideal self might have his running shoes by the door and wake up early every morning to do a 30-minute jog, rain or shine. There are many tiny habits associated with this: making sure the running shoes are where they're meant to be, setting the alarm, actually getting up, showering when home again, tracking the daily route…

Step 4: Bring those disciplines to life.

And here's where the self-discipline comes in. You already know that all these little things add up to the big thing you want. So you can shelve the big goal for now and focus only on the small stuff. Make sure you get up on time. Got it? Great. Now, go and put your running shoes on. You might not want to, but you do it anyway. That's as big as this mountain is, in this moment. You do it. Great. Now, open the door and take your first step. Great.

Self-discipline is the simplest thing in the world, but it sure isn't easy. Expect that you'll struggle and resist. Be glad for the opportunity to strengthen your willpower and determination. Never assume that you're not supposed to be uncomfortable. Embrace discomfort as a sign that you're growing and press on, acting before you give yourself the chance to come up with excuses and doubts.

Then, once you've done that, do it again. And again.

Habits gain their full force the more you do them. Rejoice in that—every time you perform a habit, it grows stronger. Little triumphs accrue and become big ones. Luckily for you, you don't have to pay attention to the big ones. Just get up. Just put your shoes on. You can think about tomorrow's tasks tomorrow. The more you practice, the sooner you'll get to that marvelous state of mind where it feels wrong *not* to do your habit. At that point, your goal is already rushing toward you, and it will happen seamlessly and naturally as an obvious consequence of the life you've set up.

Let's return to our example of weight loss. With daily, consistent action, you go month by month, slowly racking up the pounds. In a year (or two or three) you hit your 100-pound weight loss goal. The best part? You don't have to drop the habits that got you there. It's more than likely they've become a part of you.

You can look at the end goal and feel the accomplishment of knowing precisely what it took to get there. Every moment of discomfort. Every scrap of willpower. Every doubt and fear. Every moment of pleasure passed up. You'll look at yourself, having achieved your goal, and feel something that's more powerful than any specific goal could ever be: the deep conviction that you are capable, that you can create the life you want, and that you are strong enough to endure anything if it means going for what you most want for yourself.

Takeaways:

- More ways to deceive the brain into doing what we want? Of course.
- Recall that we are driven by the pleasure principle. And so we should take a deeper look to see what we can do about it. It turns out that we can manipulate the pleasure principle a bit by starkly

laying out the pleasures and pains associated with certain actions and changing your perspective on them. For any self-disciplined behavior, you would focus on the pains associated with no action and the benefits associated with action. This is another way of bringing awareness to the consequences of your action and using your rational brain.

- The physical environment we work or think in has a massive effect on our self-discipline. It can either help or hurt us, but it will always have an impact. Whatever we don't want to do, keep that out of your environment or make it more difficult to attain or reach. Humans take the path of least resistance whenever possible, so make that path the one that you want. Whatever you want to do more of, make it so that you cannot avoid it in your physical environment. Again, this seems simple, but it's still not easy.
- Shift your focus from the outcome and onto the process. An outcome is an end goal, while the process is the daily actions and habits that lead to that

outcome. This makes you focus on what you have control over, not something in the far-off future, which we already know the brain has trouble caring about. So fixate on the consistent daily actions, because that's what your brain can feel and taste.

Chapter 4. Mind Shift

At a certain point, we should begin to focus on the thoughts that inhabit our brains rather than shifting the world around to suit its tendencies. This may sound akin to the *law of attraction* or simply believing in the world and thus receiving the positive energy back that you put into it. But it's not.

This is still firmly within the realm of neuroscience, because changing your thoughts is the beginning of neuroplasticity, the process through which our brains adapt, learn, and change according to the stimulus that it receives.

The entire school of thought on neuroplasticity is centered around Hebbian theory, named after its inventor, neuroscientist David Hebb. Word for word, *Hebb's axiom* states the following:

> When an axon of cell A is near enough to excite a cell B and repeatedly or persistently takes part in firing it, some growth process or metabolic change takes place in one or both cells such that A's efficiency, as one of the cells firing B, is increased.

Put more simply, "cells that wire together, fire together." If a group of cells tends to light up together over an extended period of time, the more consistently and frequently they'll continue to do so. Likewise with habits, thoughts, decisions, reactions, behaviors, and anything else that the brain can notice patterns and trends in. The more frequently that they occur together, the more they are likely to keep occurring, because the brain begins creating neural records to save time and energy.

Sometimes this is good, and sometimes this is astoundingly bad, as anyone who has tried to shake a bad habit can attest to. Also, remember the "use it or lose it" corollary: if certain neural pathways don't get used, the brain eventually filters them out, including those that encourage positive behavior.

What's the point of mentioning Hebb's axiom? It is to demonstrate that our thoughts and internal monologue have *real power*. Whatever we end up telling ourselves time after time ends up reflecting reality. It's not just a coincidence. Better yet, this is something we actually have control over.

Our brains change according to what they're most familiar with—what happens the most in our lives. For neuroplasticity to take effect the way we want it to, we need to change the nature of our thoughts and even our approach toward self-discipline. Over time, this is something that makes self-discipline a natural part of our daily lives, rather than something to be forced into.

This chapter is all about the ways that we talk to ourselves and whether they are helpful or not.

What Did You Say to Me?

Naturally, shifting our mindsets begins with the internal monologue we use. The concept of self-talk (what we tell ourselves about ourselves, the world, and our place in it) is wide-ranging. Frankly, this can and does fill many books in itself. For our purposes, we will address it mostly in the context of becoming more self-disciplined and motivated into action.

When we embark on an arduous task, the people around us will invariably cheer us on and tell us that we can do it. However, our self-talk is typically filled with doubt and fear. As we just learned, this is going to program your brain into a lack of discipline and self-belief. So what if we started talking to ourselves as our friends do?

Self-administered pep talk has been found to be incredibly advantageous to building up self-discipline and motivation. However, there's probably a more optimal way than just telling yourself, "I can do this!" Right?

British professor Andrew Lane answered this question with the British Broadcasting Corporation (BBC). More than 44,000 people took part in the study, a much larger sample size than your average research experiment. Lane and the BBC were trying to determine whether there was a certain psychological tactic or ability that was most linked to improved performance—and, consequently, which motivational method was the best.

The BBC tested three different motivational methods and applied them to one of four different parts of a certain task in a competitive online game against a computer opponent. During the game, participants were given video "interventions" by sprinter and Olympic gold medalist Michael Johnson. These interventions tested three different motivational methods:

- *Self-talk or inner dialogue*: These were encouragements for the participants to verbally cheer themselves on—for example, "I will do better on this step the next time" or "I'm going to win this contest."

- *Imagery or visualization*: The subjects were told to make mental pictures of themselves completing each step and reaching the finish line. For example, they'd imagine themselves doing better at a certain task they were working on or see themselves celebrating after they'd improved their results.

- *"If-then" planning*: This method involved telling the subjects to execute a certain course of action to deal with setbacks that might come up in the course of their trial. For example, "If I find myself getting physically tired trying to maintain a certain speed, then I will try to do fewer steps over a certain period and try to be consistent rather than quick."

The researchers used these different interventions during four different aspects of the game:

- process (actual gameplay)
- instruction (being told what to play)
- arousal control (keeping the players' emotions under control)
- outcome (the final result)

As the game was in progress, participants would receive prompts that paired the method with each aspect in efforts to improve their performance. So for example, at some point during the game, Michael Johnson would pop on screen and instruct the player to tell themselves (self-talk) that they could do a certain function better (process). Or he'd tell the player to imagine (imagery) themselves beating their best score (outcome). All in all, sixteen such combinations were tested. Researchers then gauged how much each specific intervention improved the players' performance.

Four types of intervention were determined to be the most effective:

- *Self-talk ("I can do it!") during the outcome (final result)*: Participants were prompted to verbally say to themselves that they were going to finish their exercise with a positive result—for example, "I'm going to beat my high score." They spoke their end ambitions out loud at the end of the game.

- *Self-talk ("I can do it!") during the process (actual gameplay)*: Participants were prompted to verbalize their goals to perform better at certain smaller tasks within the game—for example, "I'm going to react to that visual cue more quickly this time." Whereas the last bit was about speaking out their end goal, this prompt encouraged them to speak about processes within the game while it was being played.

- *Imagery (mental pictures) during the outcome (final result)*: Like self-talk/outcome, the players were encouraged to concentrate on their successful completion of the game. But instead of speaking it out loud, they were told to make a mental picture of themselves attaining success—perhaps a picture of them celebrating, pumping their fists in the air, or some other end-of-game act.

- *Imagery (mental pictures) during the process (actual gameplay)*: Again, players were asked to envision themselves successfully completing a task within the game itself—to imagine a picture of themselves achieving a smaller part of gameplay with better results.

The results were a strong indicator of the power of self-affirmation in the midst of a task—especially self-talk, which was actually found to be the most successful tactic no matter what phase of the game the players were in. Although the imagery or visualization method also showed positive results, it didn't quite beat the positive effect that out-loud verbalization had on the players. Just voicing empowering and encouraging thoughts to yourself was incredibly effective.

What's interesting and slightly surprising is that the best self-talk wasn't anything special or even so deep. They were merely surface-level reminders of what to focus on, what was at stake, and what people wanted to achieve. Imagine how powerful these reminders would be if they were your natural way of approaching the world via neuroplasticity.

Since the benefits of self-talk are proven, what specific strategies should we use? The BBC study showed that self-talk and imagery (a type of visual self-talk) regarding a task's performance and the final outcome worked the best. This translates into encouraging and positive reinforcement before, during, and after the performance of the task.

What does this sound like for our purposes, coming from ourselves and not Michael Johnson?

- I'm going to eat healthier this time (during the task's performance).

- I'm going to spend 10 more minutes on the treadmill (during the task's performance).

- I will eat only half this meal and save the rest for dinner (during the task's performance).

- I will drink three liters of water today (ideal outcome).

- I will walk 15,000 steps every day this week (ideal outcome).

- I'm going to garden for two hours (ideal outcome).

Become your own best cheerleader and voice exactly what you want to happen. After all, if you repeat it enough, you will start to reprogram yourself to believe that that's the reality. If you audibly repeat (or visualize) your expectations to ace a biology final, win a decathlon, or land a dream client, you're fortifying your thinking pattern with clear statements of purpose.

An underrated portion of self-disciplined self-talk is that we must know what we want to occur before we can speak it. With self-talk, you're dealing with the here and now and where that's going to take you in the near term. It brings clarity to our actions whereas before we might have been acting without a clear purpose.

Repeated self-talk is a powerful motivator, and as with most of the suggestions this book offers, it can have real physiological effects on the discipline wiring of your brain.

Recent research on what is motivating to hear *from* others might provide even more guidance on the type of self-talk we can and should use. Professors Jacqueline and Milton Mayfield of Texas A&M University have studied motivation for nearly three decades, and they describe the most effective motivational talk and speeches as containing three main elements.

First, they talk about "uncertainty-reducing language," which is when specific, actionable directions are given. "All you need to do is X and Y and watch out for Z!" To ourselves, this becomes, "Okay, I just need to drink more water today, spend 45 minutes in the gym later, and not eat sweets."

Second is "empathetic language," which shows a degree of understanding and concern for other people's needs and desires. When you validate people's feelings, they will feel heard and appreciated. "I hear you. I know it's hard. You must be suffering a lot with it. I appreciate you." To ourselves, this becomes, "This is hard, no doubt. Not everyone does this. I have to suffer for what I want, and nothing is supposed to come easy."

Third and finally, the Mayfields articulated "meaning-making language," which explains why a task is important and the overall impact and benefits that the task is integral to. This is a statement of purpose and a reminder of why you care. "You're an important part of our message in reaching the underprivileged youth!" To ourselves, this becomes, "Just remember, I'm doing this for the starving children."

They argue that an effective motivational message should include all three of these elements. Clearly, this will be beneficial in how we talk to ourselves as well. In short order, this type of self-talk keeps us on track, defines exactly what we should be doing, makes us feel appreciated, and reminds us of what's at stake. Combined with the positive affirmations and goal statements from earlier, your mindset is bound to shift and hopefully become differently wired permanently.

Know Your Style

Beyond all the positivity that might make some of you feel like you are treating yourselves like children, there's another way to mentally make self-discipline easier.

It comes through knowing which style of discipline suits you best, but to be honest, there is a correct answer here. There are two primary approaches people take to self-discipline: moderation and abstinence. Each has its merits and negatives.

Let's start with the definitions of these words. According to Oxford Dictionaries, *moderation* is "the avoidance of excess or extremes." You'll have only one scoop of ice cream. You know when you're too drunk to keep drinking. You can limit yourself to one hour of television a day.

Merriam-Webster defines *abstinence* as "the habit of not doing or having something that is wanted or desirable." No ice cream allowed. No games. No television. No alcohol. No fun.

Let's start with moderation. Moderation, if you can handle it, is a strategy to have your cake and eat it too. Eating dessert in moderation is a way to enjoy sweets without going overboard. You wouldn't want to eat multiple desserts every single day, as there may be health, weight, and blood sugar consequences. But a dessert every now and then is acceptable. This is moderation in action. You've heard the maxim "everything in moderation," which generally supports the freedom to indulge without *over*indulging.

So what is the application of moderation in the self-discipline realm? If you are trying to accomplish a task, you can take breaks along the way. You can indulge in your distractions, take a walk, and even procrastinate a little bit. In moderation, you get a mental break, you refresh yourself, and then you start again, reenergized. There's a timeline, and as long as you're basically adhering to it, then all is well. Of course, it might be said that you need a decent degree of innate self-discipline to engage in this strategy. If so, you can save yourself from the pain of abstinence that others might encourage—it would probably drive you insane and not work for you.

Moderation can give you freedom—the freedom of choice and flexibility to adapt to your circumstances and desires. It's the happy medium between the extremes. You don't have to go all or nothing when you're able to find that "sweet spot" in between. Of course, this comes with a rather large caveat. If you identify with this description of moderated self-discipline, it's because you feel that you can regulate yourself well enough that indulging won't completely throw you off. Just imagine a chronic alcoholic or addict of any kind—a moderated approach probably isn't ideal for them.

That's where abstinence comes in. For those with a weaker sense of self-discipline, an inability to regain focus in a timely manner, unfamiliarity with flexing their self-discipline muscle, or simply seeking a simpler approach, abstinence is the way to go. You might be able to stop the action itself, but it may occupy your brain afterward for a detrimental amount of time.

Thus, it's easier to set a blanket rule for yourself instead of having to rein yourself in instance by instance and negotiate with your desires and impulses. When you have to keep telling yourself no, a lapse in judgment is far more likely to occur than when you already know the answer is no. Sometimes *complete lacking* provides less suffering than having to stop before you are fully satisfied. An addict needs to stay away because they lack the ability to control themselves in that environment or context, so it's easier to position themselves for success by keeping their temptations at arm's length.

Another example is so-called *screen time*. At times, it seems as if today's society has us in front of a screen at all hours of the day. We have smartphones, tablets, televisions, laptops, and e-readers, and one of them is never more than an arm's length away.

While many people *can* moderate their screen time, not everyone has that ability. If you are a gamer, you may need to give up gaming completely in order to be able to function—otherwise, the gamer can often be heard saying "just another round" or "just another five minutes!" Similarly, some people leave or give up social media for good because they know it's impossible to just hop on there for 30 seconds and push it completely out of their minds.

Abstinence, for some, is the simplest, surest, and easiest approach. You don't have the struggle of trying to *stop*, rather just *not starting*. Abstinence can also offer you freedom—freedom from tough choices and freedom from punishing yourself for trying to moderate or control your behavior and potentially failing.

What's the answer to improving self-discipline—moderation or abstinence? Should you try to pick one over the other? Which one is "better"? Is it always an either/or proposition? Is it just as easy as saying, "If you can handle it, moderation, and if not, abstinence"?

There are no easy answers to these questions. To some degree, you need to know yourself. Do you have a tendency for extremes? Do you go all-or-nothing when approaching a task or goal? Or are you able to cut yourself off at a given milestone or timepoint? How easily can you redirect your energies toward a task? Instead of answering these questions off the cuff, answer them by thinking about examples of your past behavior—only actions matter here, not intentions.

But as was stated in the beginning of this section, there is a correct choice, and I believe it to be abstinence. The process of negotiating with yourself and cutting yourself off may work from time to time, but the most failproof method is to simply not indulge at all. It's much easier to hear a flat "No" than "It depends; we'll see." The former creates proper expectations, while the latter keeps you fixated on regulating your self-discipline. The latter is distracting, and the probability that you say, "Well, just one more donut…" is *not* 0%.

Furthermore, this process of self-negotiation is the opposite of what we've discussed with neuroplasticity earlier in the chapter. An approach of moderated self-discipline obscures a consistent message of doing what needs to be done. This doesn't allow a neural habit to form or your instinct for self-discipline to develop. In other words, if we want to shape our brains to be automatically more disciplined, moderation sabotages that process because it sends mixed messages.

However, for those that take the view that all approaches are valid, consider the following: maybe we can think of this as a process. The first step would certainly be abstinence. While we work on our willpower, you can completely avoid your triggers and distractions. As we mature and develop our discipline, then we can consider moderation. This is otherwise known as going "cold turkey." You might find that you can completely control yourself after this learning period, and no further reinforcement is needed.

The opposite process (moderation to abstinence) can also be valid as a process of weaning yourself off of something. Here, the end goal would be complete abstinence. Whatever the case, know your own tendencies so that you don't set yourself up for failure.

Excuses, Excuses

Finally, we come to the most common way that our mindsets work against us. The scary part is that we don't always realize when we are doing it, but whether it is conscious or not, it is sabotaging our self-discipline.

Of course, we're talking about the instinct for making excuses to avoid action. Excuses are reflexive and instinctual ways in which we justify a lack of self-discipline and negative occurrences in general. They shift blame. Whether it's your fault or not, your initial impulse is often to find a way to deflect responsibility onto anything but you. This is obviously neural programming that we must utilize neuroplasticity to rewrite, and not just for self-discipline purposes.

"It's the copy machine's fault," "The other driver was moving too slow," "The reading material was too hard to understand," or "The ring (from *Lord of the Rings*) was supposed to prevent me from aging."

But here's the thing; excuses are categorically lies. It's a harsh truth that needs to be exposed in order for you to become more accountable and disciplined. Not just 99% of excuses, and not just the ones that other people use. *All* of them are lies that deprive you of your ability to get where you want to go.

Of course, there are always *reasons* things go wrong, but you'll read soon how vastly reasons differ from excuses.

We think of excuses as things we tell other people—parents, bosses, teachers, spouses, police officers—to protect our image or standing. And they are. When you tell excuses to other people, you're not necessarily hurting yourself. Others may grow annoyed at you and question your sense of responsibility, but that can be somewhat overcome.

But the people we make the most excuses to, almost without exception, are ourselves. While we tell excuses to others so we don't look bad in their eyes, we tell excuses to ourselves to protect our own ego and self-esteem. This is by far the more important function of constant excuses, and unfortunately, it leads to living in a fantasy world where any reason for toughness is simply excused away.

To be more specific, this is when excuses become a *defense mechanism*, which was first coined in the setting of psychoanalytic therapy. Over time, it became so recognized and prevalent that it's part of our daily language.

Defense mechanisms are unconscious, psychological reactions that rationalize or ease our anxiety. They protect us from the unpleasantness of confronting our weaknesses and flaws, such as a lack of self-discipline or extreme laziness. They guard us and make us feel better about ourselves.

Excuses are refusing to keep going when the going gets tough. Excuses are when you get knocked down and find a reason to stay down. *Excuses are giving up*.

Generally, if the first priority of what you're saying is to make clear how you are *not* involved, you're using an excuse, *which is a lie*. It's an easy habit to slip into unconsciously. Once you figure out that it feels great to not have to take responsibility for yourself, you'll start using it more and more until you can't tell the difference between the excuse and reality.

The consequences of constant excuses are something Professor Sean McCrea of the University of Konstanz, Germany, calls *self-handicapping*. It is aptly named because that's exactly what making excuses is: reinforcing your belief in your *inability* to do something. What's worse is that they can also reduce your motivation to work harder in the future.

So are there legitimate *reasons* that things can go wrong?

Telling the difference between an *excuse* and a *reason*, admittedly, can be tricky. In general, it comes down to one's ability to take responsibility for whatever they contribute—or fail to contribute—to a failed effort or mistake.

Excuses are intended to shift blame and allow us to give up. To use an excuse is to live in one's own weakness and helplessness. Reasons, on the other hand, focus squarely on our own actions, behaviors, and decision-making. They reinforce responsibility and lead more directly to possible change. Reasons are when you don't give up and you make the effort to push through your pain.

Of course, this doesn't mean that external factors *never* play a part in real reasons; there are always elements outside our immediate control that can affect an outcome. But a legitimate reason centers our own roles in the situation and acknowledges the mistakes or misjudgments we made that prevented optimal results from happening. They spotlight the control we have in a situation. Although admitting one's shortcomings can seem like a failing, it makes it easier to diagnose what's going wrong and make adjustments in the future. Excuses simply don't bring that kind of information or toughness to light.

Let's say you arrived late for an important meeting. Perhaps the culprits were a combination of heavy traffic, bad weather, or a personal phone call that went longer than you expected and kept you from getting ready. There are two ways you can present this. You could bemoan the fact that the weather, traffic, and call are out of your control—these are excuses. Or you could say you didn't consult traffic reports, weather reports, or set a boundary on the length of the phone call—these are reasons.

Will giving reasons guarantee that you'll escape others' temporary scorn or mental judgment? Not necessarily. But taking responsibility and emphasizing your agency in the matter is what transforms you from someone who gets knocked down and waits for help into someone who gets knocked down and finds a way to claw themselves up. In the end, you are the only one who can force yourself to keep going when it gets difficult.

Making excuses isn't always a deliberate thing. Some of these mindsets are classic personality types that we're all familiar with to an cxtent. Others are patterns of thought that we don't easily recognize. All of them conspire to make us delay, procrastinate, or simply refuse to do something. But they're also correctable.

We'll focus on five of the more common ones.

The Perfectionist. This is someone who only acknowledges results if everything goes exactly as they planned. There can be no deviation whatsoever. The Perfectionist takes a stark "all-or-nothing" approach to what they see done: either everything is right or absolutely nothing gets done. And of course, you can bet the standards of a Perfectionist are frequently impossible to meet. They'll have an absolute floor of expectation—if that minimum level of accomplishment isn't met, the entire project is a waste. So why bother?

Of course, accomplishments and goals are never binary perfect/terrible. If this is you, think of efforts in terms of a "dial," where all efforts are simply measured in levels of intensity. You might be going at 85%, 50%, or 3%—but you're doing *something* instead of shutting down if things aren't perfectly executed. Something is *always* better than nothing. If you don't come out of the gate stronger than anyone else and do everything perfectly, well, the words *improvement*, *learning*, and *progress* should be important for you.

The Intimidated. People with this mindset have some commonalities with the Perfectionist in that they use an "ideal condition" to gauge the effectiveness of their efforts. But the Intimidated is more gripped with fear than the Perfectionist. They're afraid they've overshot their ability and have taken on more than they can handle. The Intimidated is driven by a consumptive fear of the unknown and the prospect of total failure. Not only will the results be bad, but they'll also be downright disastrous—the cake in the oven won't just burn; you'll set the entire kitchen on fire.

To tame the Intimidated and overcome your terror of what might happen, the answer's very simple: research. Consider the worst-case scenario in your efforts: what would truly define utter catastrophe? Write the answer down and make whatever plans you need to avoid that terrible event from unfolding—and then get to work.

Remember too that failure is something to *learn* from. Just allowing yourself to be defined by failure, without trying to figure out the adjustments you could make to achieve a better result, is a lifelong recipe for eternal procrastination. Resist the urge to overthink and over-analyze in advance and risk "analysis paralysis"—just start something.

The Environment Blamer. People with this mindset are completely at the mercy of their surroundings. They believe they have no input or control about what happens. Life to them is merely a sequence of things that happen to them, not the accomplishments they make. Their belief that outside forces are always conspiring against them leads them to focus only on the external and not at all on their own internal abilities or contributions. This is especially helpful when they're trying to evade responsibility.

To change the Environment Blaming mindset, simply accept accountability and realize that things don't have to happen *to you*. Understand that you have just as much ability to affect your surroundings as anyone or anything else. Nothing prevents you from doing so besides yourself. This is a matter of understanding just how much you can participate in your daily life. Question whether the environment is really the cause of your sorrows or whether it's just a convenient excuse. Like the example from earlier, traffic and weather might happen to you, but that doesn't mean you can't account for them yourself.

The Defeatist. This mindset is pessimistic. A Defeatist is certain there's no chance for success—and won't let you forget about it. They've already decided they're not going to succeed, whether they say so or not. The Defeatist uses their lack of optimism to explain their own inabilities—it's not really a reflection of the truth, just that they lack the requisite tools to do anything. More often than not, this attitude stops being an opinion and turns into a self-fulfilling prophecy: they really *will* start stinking at everything.

To change the Defeatist mindset, stop confirming your own failure. Even if it runs counter to your ideas of reality, just attack the problem you're trying to solve or the goal you're trying to achieve. Break the big task down into smaller and more manageable pieces—try to score a few "quick wins" instead of the league championship all at once. It's fair and even prudent to expect hardships or tough stretches, and it's even okay to ask for outside assistance. Just don't declare that failure is inevitable. It's never a done deal.

Excuse-making is the most temporary and fruitless method to feel better. Rather than repair faults and flaws from the ground up, an excuse is more like a Band-Aid that just obscures flaws and does little to fix them. Understanding the nature of excuses helps us see them coming before we speak them. That pause in our thinking can help us see what the *real* situation is and can open up insights into how we can positively affect them. And that leads to a tenacious character that can contend with anything that comes down the path.

Now that we understand the true purpose of excuses and why they are so unhelpful, it's time to learn a method to deal with them as they arise.

The solution isn't necessarily to deny what we're telling ourselves, as that's nearly impossible. Excuses reflect certain states of mind that we may indeed *think* we're experiencing.

Instead of denying your excuses, try to dig below the surface and find three components*: the objective truth, the undisciplined action, and the disciplined action.* Drawing a clear distinction between these three factors is what will allow you to truly understand your internal dialogue and isolate where you can choose to be tough and resilient.

For example, let's say you have an essay that's due in a few days and will require you to perform research. You have a reasonable window of time to get it completed, but you're exhausted—this is the objective truth. This is the neutral reality of the situation. You've had an extreme lack of sleep deprivation, but what will you do now? So what? Life is tough, and how will you handle it? This is where the fork in the road appears and you will make your choice about how to approach it—with self-discipline or not.

Now ask yourself what an excuse would sound like. This might be your first impulse—to come up with an excuse *not* to get started. "I could start now, but I'll do much better after I get some sleep." There's your *undisciplined action*: it's allowing you to procrastinate. Even though there might be a hint of truth, its sole purpose is to allow you to take the easy way out. It is indisputably the path of least resistance. It seems to be small and harmless, but it is actually attempting to absolve you of responsibility.

Then ask yourself what the best approach for the truth is. On the other hand, you could say, "I'm tired, but if nothing else I can do a few small things right now to get the paper going. I could make a rough outline that'll make this paper easier to navigate when I'm more refreshed." That's a *disciplined action*. It is recognizing what the right and most effective choice is instead of the easy choice. It doesn't demand that you exhaust yourself, but it ensures that you set yourself up for success.

Often, it's only when we engage in this type of role-playing that we can understand we are even making an excuse. You're not required to *reject* the conditions that make up your mentally weak conclusions. No, it's not about becoming a relentless machine in the face of all adversity. Step by step, it's just about realizing that you have many choices and that the choices that lead to self-discipline are just a slight pivot away.

In a sense, whatever you make an excuse about is something that belongs on your to-do list. It's exactly what you should focus your attention on. If you think you don't have time, then you've probably got a time management problem. If you like to say that you're just unlucky, learn about people who have had good luck. If you feel that you are singled out for negative treatment from a supervisor, then you may very well need to improve your office social skills. We can move forward only when we realize that excuses are lies.

Takeaways:

- According to neuroscience, our thoughts, behaviors, actions, and habits become more natural the more we have them. So we must address the first part of that list—our thoughts. The mindset and approach we have toward self-discipline can have a drastic impact on how well we can practice it. That's Hebb's axiom, which is that cells that fire together wire together.

- The most obvious starting place is with self-talk, which is our internal dialogue. It can empower or disempower us; it will affect us one way or the other. There are specific types of self-talk that are motivating for self-discipline, and they are exactly what you think they would be. The best ones are about the ideal outcomes of what you want and about your intentions and what you will do.

- Another mindset to understand and set in stone is what your style of discipline is: either moderation or abstinence. For our purposes, abstinence is preferred because that's what makes the cells fire and wire together. This would mean that the brain would eventually begin to realize that no means no, and it would be your natural reaction and instinct.

- Let's get this out of the way upfront: excuses are lies. Excuses are the very epitome of giving up in the face of adversity, because excuses create a reality where adversity doesn't exist. They are the easy way out and lead you down a path of learned helplessness and playing the victim.

- Common excuse patterns include playing the perfectionist, blaming the environment, being too intimidated, and being a defeatist. A method to defeat these excuse patterns, as well as any other excuses in general, is to look for three components of your situation: *the objective truth, the undisciplined action, and the disciplined action*. Finding the separation between these perspectives is how you can realize which path you should take.

Chapter 5. Creating Space and Calm

In earlier chapters, we learned some sneaky ways to use the brain's tendencies against itself. If the brain wants a mixture of speed and pleasure, then by golly, we're going to give it speed and pleasure, but in a way that serves us.

But it's helpful to have even more tools so that you don't always need to cater to the brain's childish ways. Here, we move to a set of tactics and approaches that are about soothing and calming the brain. Ideally, we want to make the brain less reactive overall. We want to blunt both the speed and strength of our emotions that can lead to self-sabotaging behaviors and a lack of self-discipline. In other words, this means that there will be less imbalance between the two brains (logical prefrontal brain and the emotional limbic brain).

Having a calmer brain will simply make many of the tactics in this book unnecessary; they suffice in the short-term, while ridding the brain of emotional spikes is a lifelong journey.

Delay, Delay, Delay

Although the brain can't be said to be a muscle that grows in response to repetitive exercise, the brain adapts in the same way through repetitive behaviors and thoughts. The first time you step foot in a gym, every single push-up or pull-up is going to be a struggle—but then it gets better and easier. Likewise, the first time you exercise self-discipline and delay gratification, you might feel like you're going to rip your hair out—and then after a while, you wonder what all the fuss was about.

Humans are hardwired to want things immediately. This is called instant gratification and it is an extremely powerful force that winds its way through all aspects of life. It's one of the most universal and predictable causes of human behavior.

Again, that pesky pleasure principle comes up again. This principle is the driving force that implores you to satisfy your needs, wants, and urges. These can be as basic as breathing or as complex as the desire for a new iPhone. Instant gratification is the desire to satisfy these needs and wants without delay. This is the opposite of what those with mental toughness practice—*delayed gratification*.

Delayed gratification is the practice of waiting for what you want. Waiting or abstaining can be incredibly difficult, but ultimately it trains you to separate yourself from your emotional brain and lock it in a cage when need be.

In the 1960s, a Stanford professor conducted a well-known psychological experiment dubbed *the marshmallow experiment*. He gave a series of children a difficult choice: eat one marshmallow now or wait a short time and receive two marshmallows. Predictably, many children chose to eat the single marshmallow immediately. Some children tried to wait but quickly gave in and ate the marshmallow. It was a small percentage of the children that were able to successfully wait and receive the second marshmallow.

The outcome of the experiment is not surprising. What is surprising is what happened to these children when they grew up. The children that were able to wait to receive the second marshmallow grew up to be more successful, were less likely to be obese or have substance abuse issues, had higher academic marks and test scores, and generally had better performance on other measures of life success.

The marshmallow test ended up being a microcosm for life at large. Success and goal achievement typically come down to being able to choose the pain of discipline over the easier choice of rest or distraction. These children, at a very young age, were exhibiting self-discipline. They were able to choose the pain of mental toughness and set themselves up to face the realities of life.

Think of it this way: if children were able to do it, you can certainly do it, or at least improve in your capacity for it. Making the choice to forego short-term pleasure in order to gain increased long-term satisfaction and rewards is the very spirit of building the skill of self-discipline.

Getting into the habit of delaying gratification gives you more control over your life, decisions, and habits. All it takes is waiting for a marshmallow later rather than having one right now—realize that nothing is lost by waiting (despite what your brain will try to tell you). It is deceptively easy to start thinking in terms of delaying your gratification.

First, set yourself up for success. Get rid of all reminders of instant gratification. It sounds simple, but if you are constantly surrounded by temptation, it can be tricky. For most people, this will consist of changing their environment to hide, or remove, the temptations. The more difficult it becomes to access temptations, the less likely you will be to indulge in them. Staying focused and on-task when problems arise is in large part a matter of the type of environment you construct for yourself.

This is the reason that health experts often recommend placing healthy food choices in the front of your refrigerator or out on the kitchen counter while hiding or throwing away unhealthy choices.

Second, after you have adjusted your environment so you stop fixating on instant gratification, you need to focus on not making excuses for your behavior. We need to dramatically shift the internal monologue you use to justify instant gratification, even that which can seemingly be benign.

"I'm feeling a little hungry. Maybe I'll just eat some of these potato chips before I meet Carol for dinner in 10 minutes."

"This is a brand-new episode of my favorite show! I better watch it right now instead of cleaning the kitchen. It might not come on again this evening."

If thoughts like these have crossed your mind, you are trying to justify instant gratification instead of waiting for what you know is the better behavior. So let's address it head-on: there is *never* a good excuse for indulging in temptations. In reality, we use similar excuses and defense mechanisms so frequently that it's hard for us to know the difference sometimes between a real and imagined justification. So let's take our thoughts and adjust them—we will change the internal dialogue with a simple nod to self-discipline.

"I'm feeling a little hungry. Maybe I'll just eat some of these potato chips before I meet Carol for dinner in 10 minutes."

Becomes:

"I lack the self-discipline to delay eating for 20 more minutes."

"This is a brand-new episode of my favorite show! I better watch it right now instead of cleaning the kitchen. It might not come on again this evening."

Becomes:

"I lack the self-discipline to clean the kitchen."

If you find that you are indulging in instant gratification, simply insert "I lack the self-discipline to…" in front of what you are avoiding. It creates a black and white judgment on yourself. It's a bit startling when we see stark reality stripped of any defenses. Instead of proactively making excuses for yourself, you may be able to delay gratification by proactively vilifying yourself.

Another effective way to delay gratification is to invest your mental bandwidth into the future. To do this, consider every action through the lens of what you are likely to gain in the future. Sure, going to the gym tonight is tough, but you will be fitter in the future and possibly increase your lifespan. Choosing to work on your big presentation now, instead of heading out to happy hour with friends, may seem torturous, but you will be more prepared during the event and might even score a promotion.

It's all about zooming out on your timeline and seeing the bigger picture. This is when you can gain perspective on what you are delaying for. This reminder, in and of itself, may be enough to motivate you to move forward. You are always weighing the future that you want against your present desires and temptations.

Finally, simply ask yourself why you want to engage in something five times.

This tactic is all about getting to the root of your impulse for instant gratification. You're actually asking the same or similar question five times in a row, and you'll be surprised to learn that, each time, you just might pull out a different answer than before. You're forcing yourself to justify why an impulse should win out over self-discipline five times. That's pretty tough, and this repetition in itself can be enough to make you stop. At the end of the process, you'll either be able to answer *why* sufficiently, or you'll come to the conclusion that it was an impulse not worth partaking in.

Impulses and the urge for instant gratification are almost never thought through or founded on deep analysis, so you wouldn't expect to be able to answer *why* more than once or twice. Thus, only if you can answer *why* a few times does it pass the sniff test of importance or urgency. Practically speaking, what does this look like? Suppose you have an impulse to break your budget and buy a new sweater.

Why do you want it?
I like it.
Why do you want it?
It's a great price. (This is as far as an impulse will probably carry you.)

Why do you want it?
No real reason other than wanting it...
Why do you want it?
Looks cool?
Why do you want it?
I guess I don't, really.

Once you've asked yourself *why* five times, in five different ways, you have distilled the main pros and cons of why you should or shouldn't buy the shirt. And really, you've come up with nothing to justify the impulse. If this was really a shirt that you needed in some way, you'd be able to come up with better answers, such as "Because my other shirt ripped" or "I have a wedding coming up" or "I want to look nice for a date!" In those instances, you are *not* dealing with an impulse masquerading as a need—it's an actual need. There would be no reason to delay the gratification.

Even if it doesn't bring you to the point where you realize you can't answer *why* five times (which is a red flag), at least it will force you to stop and think about your decisions. Whatever the case, you've become more mindful and disciplined in your daily life.

Hopefully clarity and awareness of your future self will help stop your impulses. The truth is, we very rarely get something for nothing in life. You will undoubtedly need to endure pain, deprivation, and discomfort in the present. But that's a temporary state.

Keep Your Mind

A calm and focused mind is the only mind that has the possibility of being self-disciplined. If you're walking through life overthinking and constantly stressed, it's a wonder that you can exercise self-discipline at all. We turn to the practice of mindfulness in another approach to calm down the brain overall and make it so that your natural state of mind is rational and nonreactive.

Mindfulness is the practice of purposefully focusing all of your attention on the current moment and being completely aware of yourself, your emotions, and your thoughts.

It can keep your mind from overthinking and running amok, which is the precursor to a lapse in self-discipline. The person who is aware of their thoughts as they are happening is far more likely to keep it together versus the person who is unaware of what is happening in the present.

You might be consumed by thoughts of past regrets or by anxiety of a future that may never occur. Being in these states makes it easy to slip. It's not so much that donuts will appear in your mouth if you're unaware and distracted, but you won't properly be able to assess whether you are thinking with your primal or logical brain.

In some sense, this is going to be our biggest enemy to self-discipline. Our brains are working against us, but the lives we lead are as well. Most of us face constant stress and anxiety in varying degrees. It doesn't have to be debilitating; it simply has to take us off the path of presence and emotional stability.

Mindfulness is a handy solution to all of those problems. As mentioned, it is quite literally the practice of emptying your mind—most frequently on your breathing, for example. Of course, it is difficult to let go of things because you feel that you must ensure that they don't fall through the cracks. The two worst things you can do for yourself are focusing on past events that you can't change or focusing on present events and comparing them with your future. One is long gone, and one has yet to happen. Neither should be your concern.

It will feel distressing at first because people who are stressed or overwhelmed constantly feel that they have too much on their plate to ever stop churning. This makes everything worse; when you're continuously moving 24/7, this gives your brain and body very little time to recharge. As we've mentioned at various points in this book, a stressed brain is the opposite of a disciplined brain.

Let go of the past, the future, and even what you're feeling in the present moment.

Anything that you can potentially fixate on, just drop it and trust that it will be right where you left it in 30 minutes. Make a list of these thoughts before you attempt to achieve mindfulness, and rest assured that the world will not end in the meantime.

Your focus should be only on what is happening now in your physical surroundings. Let go of what might happen later, what happened earlier, and all thoughts of the present. The only thing that matters is your breathing, your physical sensations, and the noises, sounds, smells, and sights around you.

Although it is most common to sit during meditation, you may choose to kneel or stand. Just make sure that whatever you pick is comfortable for you to remain for 30 minutes. You can't empty your mind if your body is suffering. Ease yourself from any tension that you might feel by relaxing your body as a whole and focusing your mind on the task at hand—*nothingness.*

Make sure that you aren't bent over so that the air you breathe is easily accessible to your lungs. Inhale through your nose. Make sure that your breaths are deep and slow. In doing so, you will allow the air that you take in to go directly to your stomach, ensuring that you're breathing the correct way for the purposes of your meditation practice.

Your mind may begin to wander from your breath, but don't chastise yourself—this is only natural. However, during the times that wandering takes place, forgive, forget, move forward, and focus on your breathing. This will help you regain focus rather than wrestle with your wayward thoughts. You'll notice how easy it is for your anxieties to try to hijack your peace of mind and constantly jump into the mental space you've created. Instead of engaging with them and unfolding these thoughts, observe them and just let them go, then return to your breathing. We're not necessarily trying to quiet our minds, but rather focus all our chatter onto one thing.

For some of us with noisier minds, you might find it more helpful to focus on a physical sensation. For instance, some will balance a cup of water on their heads (or simply hold it) because this is an act that requires the utmost concentration. Coincidentally, this is why many feel that running and other repetitive motions can create a meditative state. You can also move through your body, limb by limb, and feel the sensations present in each part.

Let go. Enjoy the break from the outside pressures you face daily. Reboot your brain and eliminate all the clutter that was preventing you from thinking clearly or being self-aware.

If it sounds too simplistic to be correct, you're in for a surprise. At the core, this is where mindfulness comes from. Your brain gains a rare reprieve from the proverbial mouse on a wheel. Your body is able to reset ever so slightly to a state of homeostasis and relaxation. You are able to gain perspective on your anxieties from earlier and understand that you are not forced to be overwhelmed—it was your choice all along. And most of all, you are now mentally in a position to make your best, self-disciplined decisions.

Again, if it sounds too simplistic, rest assured, studies have confirmed that the practice of meditation does indeed have a real effect. MRI scans were taken of volunteers before and after they participated in an eight-week mindfulness course, the results of which make a strong case for meditation being a useful tool for "strengthening" the areas of the brain that are responsible for executive functions and thus self-discipline—specifically the dorsolateral prefrontal cortex, the anterior cingulate cortex, and the orbitofrontal cortex, which are regions all firmly within our logical brain.

Moreover, meditation was shown to shrink the amygdala, a major part of the emotional limbic brain and also the center of the fight-or-flight instinct. All of this means that those who practice mindfulness are less susceptible to fear, emotional impulses, and stress. Self-discipline is often sabotaged by emotional impulses and stress, so keeping these under control is helpful in setting the conditions for willpower.

On top of that, scans showed that the gray matter in the prefrontal cortex had become noticeably denser. The gray matter growth wasn't isolated to just the prefrontal cortex. The brain structure located behind the frontal lobe—the anterior cingulate cortex—also became denser with meditation practice. This brain area has been associated with functions having to do with self-regulation, such as monitoring attention conflicts and allowing for greater cognitive flexibility. In other words, meditation can both reduce the feelings and emotions that make us lose self-control and increase our ability to manage those feelings by physically improving the brain structures responsible for them.

If mindfulness isn't already a part of your daily routine, consider adding it in. It's common to hear people say that they don't have time for meditation, possibly even seeing this as scheduling a time to be unproductive. But if meditating for a few minutes a day can make you more capable of carrying out your intentions just as you want, the increased focus and discipline while you are active will more than make up for a few minutes of inactivity.

The Master of Discomfort

Ultimately, what we may be looking for when we think about self-discipline is hardening ourselves and gaining the ability to simply push through tasks more often than not.

The brain can be tricked, mindsets can be shifted, and we can manipulate our surroundings all we want. At the core, we still need to engage in something we find at least slightly annoying or uncomfortable. Evidence is everywhere. For instance…

"Lose weight without the diet and exercise!"

"Think positively and you'll get whatever you want, without effort!"

"Follow this plan and you'll only have to work four hours in a week!"

In our modern consumer world, where marketing and advertising compete for our attention and our money at every turn, the name of the game is offering something for nothing. Abs without crunches. Money in the bank without breaking a sweat. Knowledge without studying too hard.

Products like this are successful because they tap into humankind's collective desire to avoid discomfort at all costs. We all have the dream of living in a world where we get everything we want without trying too hard or being scared or making any sacrifice. Otherwise, what's the lottery for?

However, as we've seen, a massive part of success in life comes down to self-discipline, and self-discipline is at its core made of nothing but the willingness to endure discomfort. In other words, there are no shortcuts, no easy life hacks, no quick tricks. Success in the bigger picture belongs to those who have mastered the ability to tolerate a degree of distress and uncertainty and who can thrive in situations of sacrifice in service of something bigger than their immediate pleasure in the moment.

Self-discipline = being uncomfortable. No tips or tactics needed.

We all want to grow and achieve, but the truth is that the state of growth is inherently an uncomfortable one. Evolving feels uncertain and risky at times, and it certainly requires us to give up immediate pleasures and old, easy habits. Growth and development is about expanding, risking, exploring. It cannot be done without leaving the security of the old behind. And sometimes, change requires pain, as the old dies and the new is still small and uncertain.

Self-discipline is not required for the easy parts of life. It takes no effort or special technique to enjoy what we already enjoy. But if we want to productively approach the rest of life, we need to develop the self-discipline to work with the things we don't enjoy. Rather than thinking of pain, discomfort, and uncertainty as roadblocks in our way to pleasure and success, we understand that they're simply a part of life, and if we manage them well, we can unlock even bigger pleasures.

There is a great paradox in learning to not just tolerate but embrace discomfort. Practicing being uncomfortable doesn't sound like much fun, and it isn't. But it is a skill that will reap far more rewards in the long-term than merely chasing fleeting pleasures or shifting fancies in each moment.

Simply, we practice self-discipline and familiarity with discomfort because we respect that life contains an inevitable amount of discomfort. We know that in gaining a new perspective on the things we don't really want to do, we actually create new opportunities for fulfillment, meaning, and pleasure. Life becomes easier, and we become stronger, almost larger than the everyday trials and troubles life can throw our way.

With self-discipline, our expectations become healthier and more in line with reality. Our work becomes more focused and purposeful and we are able to achieve more. Self-discipline is not a thing we simply decide we want or think is a good idea in theory. It's a practice that we pitch up for again and again, every day and every moment, willing to work it out in the arena of our lived experience. In other words, self-discipline is a habit in a world where the easiest thing is to take the path of least resistance or fall prey to the "succeed without trying" traps all around us.

It might seem logical at first to pursue pleasure. But if there's one thing we know with utmost certainty, it's that things *will* change around us, we *will* have to endure suffering at one point or another, and we *will* be uncomfortable and forced to face things we wish we didn't have to. If we have this knowledge, isn't it better to be prepared rather than blindly pursue a dazzling goal with no thought to what you'll do when that goal doesn't go how you planned?

Learning how to tolerate distress, uncertainty, doubt, and risk while things are okay (i.e., before these things are forced on you by life) gives you the opportunity to practice and develop your discipline so you're prepared for future discomfort. Yes, it means that walking barefoot makes you more "immune" to one day having to walk without shoes. But it also means you're less attached to needing shoes, and you feel deep down that you are more than able to respond to and endure challenges. This is an attitude of empowerment. It's looking at life's challenges head-on and deciding to accept them and respond with dignity and grit.

Practicing tolerance is a "vaccine" in that you inoculate yourself against future discomfort in general. Adversity will still bother you, but you'll move through it with the quiet confidence that it won't kill you. How can it, when you've endured it all before and only came out stronger?

You can turn your focus to maximizing pleasure and refusing to engage with pain;

or you can acknowledge that life intends to serve you heaping doses of both, and if you can prepare with maturity and wisdom, you can stay calm and ride those waves, trusting that you've developed your ability to survive.

So prepare while the going is still easy. Don't wait for life to force you to learn the lessons you must, sooner or later. Take the initiative by developing self-discipline right now. The shift is only a small one, but mentally it has great influence on how you approach yourself and life. The idea is straightforward: get more uncomfortable than you'd usually be. Give yourself the gift of the opportunity to grow stronger.

Importantly, you're not just thinking about these things or talking about them. It's not enough to "get" the concept intellectually or abstractly. One must actually have a *real lived experience* of discomfort. You need to get your hands dirty out there in the trenches of real life.

Develop self-discipline either by putting yourself in uncomfortable positions or by deliberately choosing to forgo comfortable ones. Train your will and discipline in the same way you would any other muscle: with repeated exercise. Become the person that is able to push through and do what others dread doing; become the person who can resist doing what everyone else can't resist. The way to do that? With a finely cultivated ability to tolerate discomfort and forego pleasure.

No, you are not being a masochist. You are not a glutton for punishment who wants to martyr themselves on the personal development altar and make a big show of how poorly they can treat themselves. It is actually your desire for a better, more meaningful life that moves you; it's because you ultimately want to make things easier that you are willing to have them be harder for a while.

Again, the paradox is that deliberately engaging with discomfort sometimes shows you just how insignificant it sometimes is. It allows you to enjoy the pleasures on a richer, deeper level. It's like forcing yourself to look under the bed to check for monsters. In the same way that there never is a monster, self-discipline can also teach you that doing without what you think you "need" is sometimes far easier than we think and that we're far stronger than we believed. Without giving yourself the chance to confront distress head-on, you might always cling to ideas of what you could never endure (i.e., certain the monster is still under the bed because you never gathered the courage to check).

Cold showers, going underdressed for the cold, sleeping on the floor, or foregoing food for a while don't sound like fun, but they are certainly something you can bear. They're all something that you can go through and come out the other end—intact! Afterward, take notice of how you feel. You may be surprised to note a feeling of calm confidence and achievement. Rather than being diminished by the experience, you might feel enriched, in a small way.

You can remind yourself as you endure the discomfort that, with each moment, you are making it more and more likely that you will better cope with adversity in the future. This knowledge gives you confidence and also reduces your fear of the unknown. When you can anticipate a negative outcome and be prepared for it, the future doesn't seem so threatening, and risks seem easier to manage.

You don't want to do any of it, sure. But you can. That's a skill. You *can* take cold showers. You *can* sleep on the floor. You *can* go without food. You *can* bear discomforts when they come. You can proactively manage your own fear and insecurity and get on top of it, rather than have it control you. And better yet, you are better equipped to respond in a world filled with quick fixes, distractions, and easy pleasure.

How does one actually practice all this, though? What does it look like in day-to-day life to cultivate self-discipline?

As a first step, don't dive into the deep end. Build up your confidence and your tolerance bit by bit. Perhaps you decide you'd like to stop mindless distractions like browsing online or looking at your phone constantly. Rather than throwing your phone in a lake and vowing to go offline completely, you instead ratchet up the discomfort slowly, giving yourself time to acknowledge and absorb the feeling of being able to manage. First, you decide not to keep your phone next to your bed. You notice the urge to have it anyway and notice feelings of boredom and the urge to grab it and get that easy dopamine hit.

You tell yourself, "I can do this. I'm in control. It's okay to feel uncomfortable. I'm staying with this feeling of discomfort."

And, lo and behold, you discover you can endure it. You make a habit of it. No arguing, justification, excuses, or avoidance. You simply acknowledge, "Yes, it's uncomfortable. Yes, I don't like it. But that's okay. I can do this."

Next, you inch up the discomfort. You've done the hard work of starting and you've given yourself proof that you can indeed bear discomfort. Now, you can push it a little. Perhaps you decide to whittle your mindless phone scrolling to just an hour a day. It's a small goal, but you achieve it. You feel proud of having done it. You may even notice that this pride feels better than the fleeting moment of entertainment or distraction you got from scrolling in the first place. You keep telling yourself, "I can do this."

Keep going. Gradually push yourself out of your comfort zone. Notice when you're pushing back against your decision. Sit quietly with your discomfort, whatever it looks like. It might take the form of anger or irritation. It might suddenly become very clever and try to convince you how unnecessary this all is and how you might as well cave because it doesn't matter. It might get depressed at having to engage with an emotion it feels entitled to be free of.

Simply watch all this come, and watch it go. Feel the calm you have in the wake of successfully enduring all this discomfort. Isn't it wonderful to know that you can stand calm and strong through the storm? Tell yourself, "It's okay that I'm feeling discomfort. I'm in control. It will pass."

Finally, you might start to notice interesting things happen the more you practice. Watch your discomfort and watch your growing and changing response to it. Are certain things getting easier? Are you becoming familiar with all your idiosyncratic ways of resisting discomfort internally? Say to yourself, "I am capable of sitting with discomfort and any other negative feelings that may pass. I'm watching with curiosity. I will stay here with myself and with the feeling. I can do this. I will not respond with avoidance or escape or resistance. I welcome the experience. I can do this."

Of course, the other side of learning to tolerate discomfort is not just to endure negative feelings but to deliberately put off positive ones. Self-denial is the other side of the same self-discipline coin. Many addictive behaviors have their root in our inability to forego easy pleasure in the moment and bear the reality of the moment just as it is, right now.

Flex your self-discipline muscle by learning to say no to some of your impulses and urges. Train yourself to understand that you can act, even if you don't feel like it, and you can turn down an action, even if you really feel like doing it. As above, give yourself the opportunity to notice the feeling of calm strength this gives you.

Skip eating that sweet treat you go for automatically. Turn off the TV after one episode and force yourself to stand up rather than get sucked into three more episodes. Bite your tongue rather than say something regrettable to someone. A little self-denial opens up a crucial window of opportunity in which you can pause and deliberate on your actions. Are they in line with your ultimate goals? Do you *really* need to do them? What would you gain by turning them down for once?

Self-restraint and presence of mind enhance your sense of empowerment and control. Rather than being reactive and unconscious in your habits, stop and sink into the feeling of not fulfilling every desire, not acting, not going the easy way, or abstaining. It's a counterintuitive approach, but one that only yields greater and greater rewards the more it's practiced.

Here is a brief passage from *Meditations* by the Roman emperor-philosopher Marcus Aurelius that illustrates what we lose by surrendering to discomfort (of which is no concern to him) and not taking steps toward what we want in life:

> At dawn, when you have trouble getting out of bed, tell yourself: "I have to go to work—as a human being. What do I have to complain of, if I'm going to do what I was born for—the things I was brought into the world to do? Or is this what I was created for? To huddle under the blankets and stay warm?

'But it's nicer here…'

So you were born to feel "nice"? Instead of doing things and experiencing them? Don't you see the plants, the birds, the ants and spiders and bees going about their individual tasks, putting the world in order, as best they can? And you're not willing to do your job as a human being? Why aren't you running to do what your nature demands?

'—But we have to sleep sometime…'

Agreed. But nature set a limit on that—as it did on eating and drinking. And you're over the limit. You've had more than enough of that. But not of working. There you're still below your quota. You don't love yourself enough. Or you'd love your nature too, and what it demands of you. People who love what they do wear themselves down doing it, they even forget to wash or eat.

Takeaways:

- Ultimately, our brains are reactive, fearful, angry, and highly impatient. Our natural neurophysiology cannot be denied, but it also cannot be said that we can't find ways to be less reactive, fearful, angry, and impatient. Many methods exist to calm down our brains to create space and calm, and these should be exercises that we are always working on to improve our self-discipline. This is the closest it gets to going directly against our brain's chemistry.
- We can practice delayed gratification. This is simply abstaining from an indulgence for a set period of time. It doesn't need to be necessary, but the more you can practice this feeling of deprivation and lacking, the better off you will be. A tip to help you gain perspective about your ability to delay gratification is to ask yourself *why* five times. It will soon become clear that you don't actually have a good answer for that question; it will boil down to you

simply wanting it and breaking your self-discipline. It is a stark reminder.

- Mindfulness is the act of letting go of all thoughts except one. Well, that's one definition anyway. Most of us are in a state of stress and anxiety without even knowing it. We are constantly bombarded by so much chatter and so many cries for our attention that we don't know what it is to have a calm and quiet mind. Let go and focus only on your breath, and bring your brain back to a state where it doesn't feel the need to react violently or instantly. When you are aware of your thoughts, you can control them better.

- As we've discussed, self-discipline is at its core uncomfortable, sacrificial, inconvenient, and difficult. There's no getting around that, no matter which techniques from this book that you use. And so, building your discomfort muscle and becoming comfortable with discomfort will serve you perhaps better than anything else. When you simply have the ability to put your head down and grind through what needs to be done, well, that's self-discipline. Everything else is just designed to get you to that point. Like with delayed gratification, this is something you can practice in larger increments and build up like an immunity/tolerance.

Summary Guide

Chapter 1. The Neuroscience of Self-Discipline

- The neuroscience of self-discipline is really a tale of two brains. We have one brain, our more primitive and survival-focused brain, which simply makes us react for speed. It is fearful, high-strung, and not ultimately that smart. It's the limbic system, which we can also see as a skittish cat. Then we have our rational and thinking brain, the one which is capable of analyzing information and responding for accuracy rather than speed. This brain, while not always smart, is what allows self-discipline to occur. It is the prefrontal cortex, which we can see as Mr. Albert Einstein. Einstein and the skittish cat are constantly battling each other for supremacy, and it's up to us to make sure that the cat loses more often than not.

- Another large aspect of being biologically wired against self-discipline comes in the form of the pleasure principle. This principle simply states that humans are predisposed to seeking pleasure and avoiding pain, heavily reinforced by the neurotransmitter dopamine. This process hijacks our brain and makes discipline difficult, as it is the polar opposite of the pleasure principle; it is immediate discomfort and only long-term pleasure.
- We thus come to the realization that our brains are scared and lazy. Meanwhile, self-discipline is a process that requires an amount of awareness and rational thought. One way to think about this is through the Five Second Rule, in which self-disciplined action is best done within five seconds, or else primitive emotions are able to take us off course. It kicks us into motion before our brains, which are wired for fear and laziness, hold us back.
- Finally, a note on the mindset of self-discipline. We've been through the neuroscience, but we must touch on the

concept of sacrifice. At its core, self-discipline is sacrifice and letting go. It is feeling discomfort, pushing past boundaries, and doing more than you ever did before. Those feelings, combined with deprivation, are the signs that you are on the right path.

Chapter 2. Trick the Brain

- It turns out that we need to trick the brain and work with it instead of directly battling its natural tendencies and trying to change them. Good luck with that! We need to treat the brain like an angry and grumpy infant—you can't just tell it to stop crying; you need to be strategic.
- The first strategy to trick our brains into self-discipline is to proactively consider tomorrow—in other words, your future self and how today's decisions will impact him or her. We are usually too stuck in only the present, but just like we have two brains, we have two selves we should keep in mind. So imagine and visualize your future self's life when you

are faltering or struggling with a decision. It will help keep you focused on what needs to be done for your ultimate happiness.
- Behavior chains, or if-then statements, or implementation intentions, are another method to tricking the brain. They work because they remove the choice from your hands, and thus self-disciplined behavior is almost the expectation. It works simply as "if X, then Y," where X is an everyday occurrence and Y is your desired action. The more concrete you make your intentions, the more likely they are to happen.
- Temptation bundling tricks the brain because it gives the brain the dopamine and pleasure it seeks but ties it to a self-disciplined act. Yes, this is using carrots as motivators or simply bribing yourself to set yourself into motion and stay on track. It's as easy as it sounds.
- As the brain wants pleasure as soon as possible, there are a few ways we can simulate that feeling. First is to break your desired tasks or behaviors into the

smallest components possible. This allows you to reduce the barrier to getting started and also feel a constant sense of victory. Second, we can keep track of all victories and notice how much progress is constantly being made. Third, we will also feel more motivated and disciplined if we sense that we are relatively close to completion.

Chapter 3. Trick the Brain Pt. 2

- More ways to deceive the brain into doing what we want? Of course.
- Recall that we are driven by the pleasure principle. And so we should take a deeper look to see what we can do about it. It turns out that we can manipulate the pleasure principle a bit by starkly laying out the pleasures and pains associated with certain actions and changing your perspective on them. For any self-disciplined behavior, you would focus on the pains associated with no action and the benefits associated with action. This is another way of bringing

awareness to the consequences of your action and using your rational brain.
- The physical environment we work or think in has a massive effect on our self-discipline. It can either help or hurt us, but it will always have an impact. Whatever we don't want to do, keep that out of your environment or make it more difficult to attain or reach. Humans take the path of least resistance whenever possible, so make that path the one that you want. Whatever you want to do more of, make it so that you cannot avoid it in your physical environment. Again, this seems simple, but it's still not easy.
- Shift your focus from the outcome and onto the process. An outcome is an end goal, while the process is the daily actions and habits that lead to that outcome. This makes you focus on what you have control over, not something in the far-off future, which we already know the brain has trouble caring about. So fixate on the consistent daily actions, because that's what your brain can feel and taste.

Chapter 4. Mind Shift

- According to neuroscience, our thoughts, behaviors, actions, and habits become more natural the more we have them. So we must address the first part of that list—our thoughts. The mindset and approach we have toward self-discipline can have a drastic impact on how well we can practice it. That's Hebb's axiom, which is that cells that fire together wire together.

- The most obvious starting place is with self-talk, which is our internal dialogue. It can empower or disempower us; it will affect us one way or the other. There are specific types of self-talk that are motivating for self-discipline, and they are exactly what you think they would be. The best ones are about the ideal outcomes of what you want and about your intentions and what you will do.

- Another mindset to understand and set in stone is what your style of discipline is: either moderation or abstinence. For our purposes, abstinence is preferred because that's what makes the cells fire and wire together. This would mean that the brain would eventually begin to realize that no means no, and it would be your natural reaction and instinct.

- Let's get this out of the way upfront: excuses are lies. Excuses are the very epitome of giving up in the face of adversity, because excuses create a reality where adversity doesn't exist. They are the easy way out and lead you down a path of learned helplessness and playing the victim.

- Common excuse patterns include playing the perfectionist, blaming the environment, being too intimidated, and being a defeatist. A method to defeat these excuse patterns, as well as any other excuses in general, is to look for three components of your situation: *the objective truth, the undisciplined action, and the disciplined action.* Finding the separation between these perspectives is how you can realize which path you should take.

Chapter 5. Creating Space and Calm

- Ultimately, our brains are reactive, fearful, angry, and highly impatient. Our natural neurophysiology cannot be denied, but it also cannot be said that we can't find ways to be less reactive, fearful, angry, and impatient. Many methods exist to calm down our brains to create space and calm, and these should be exercises that we are always working on to improve our self-discipline. This is the closest it gets to going directly against our brain's chemistry.
- We can practice delayed gratification. This is simply abstaining from an indulgence for a set period of time. It doesn't need to be necessary, but the more you can practice this feeling of deprivation and lacking, the better off you will be. A tip to help you gain perspective about your ability to delay gratification is to ask yourself *why* five times. It will soon become clear that you don't actually have a good answer for that question; it will boil down to you

simply wanting it and breaking your self-discipline. It is a stark reminder.
- Mindfulness is the act of letting go of all thoughts except one. Well, that's one definition anyway. Most of us are in a state of stress and anxiety without even knowing it. We are constantly bombarded by so much chatter and so many cries for our attention that we don't know what it is to have a calm and quiet mind. Let go and focus only on your breath, and bring your brain back to a state where it doesn't feel the need to react violently or instantly. When you are aware of your thoughts, you can control them better.
- As we've discussed, self-discipline is at its core uncomfortable, sacrificial, inconvenient, and difficult. There's no getting around that, no matter which techniques from this book that you use. And so, building your discomfort muscle and becoming comfortable with discomfort will serve you perhaps better than anything else. When you simply have the ability to put your head down and grind through what needs to be

done, well, that's self-discipline. Everything else is just designed to get you to that point. Like with delayed gratification, this is something you can practice in larger increments and build up like an immunity/tolerance.

Printed in Great Britain
by Amazon